Contra Costa Child Care Council
1035 Detroit Ave., Ste. 200
Concord, CA 94518

For Gramma,
who always listened

D0122010

Contra Costa Child Care Council
1035 Detroit Ave., Ste. 200
Concord, CA 94518

of related interest

Asperger's Syndrome
A Guide for Parents and Professionals
Tony Attwood
Foreword by Lorna Wing
ISBN 1 85302 577 1

Understanding and Working with the Spectrum of Autism
An Insider's View
Wendy Lawson
Foreword by Margot Prior
ISBN 1 85302 971 8

Congratulations! It's Asperger Syndrome
Jen Birch
ISBN 1 84310 112 2

Autism: An Inside-Out Approach
An Innovative Look at the 'Mechanics' of 'Autism' and its Developmental 'Cousins'
Donna Williams
ISBN 1 85302 387 6

Pretending to be Normal
Living with Asperger's Syndrome
Liane Holliday Willey
Foreword by Tony Attwood
ISBN 1 85302 749 9

Freaks, Geeks and Asperger Syndrome
A User Guide to Adolescence
Luke Jackson
Foreword by Tony Attwood
ISBN 1 84310 098 3

Demystifying the Autistic Experience

A Humanistic Introduction for Parents, Caregivers, and Educators

William Stillman

Jessica Kingsley Publishers
London and Philadelphia

First published in the United Kingdom in 2003
by Jessica Kingsley Publishers Ltd
116 Pentonville Road
London N1 9JB, England
and
325 Chestnut Street
Philadelphia, PA 19106, USA
www.jkp.com

Copyright © William Stillman 2003
Back cover photo by Tim McGowan

Second impression 2003

Library of Congress Cataloging in Publication Data
Stillman, William, 1963-
    Demistifying the autistc experience : a humanistic introduction for paretns, caregivers, and educators / William Stillman
        p. cm.
    Includes bibliographical refereences and index.
    ISBN 1-84310-726-0 (alk. paper)
    1. Autism. 2. Autism in children. I. Title.

RC553.A88 S84 2002
616.89'82--dc21   2002028651

British Library Cataloguing in Publication Data
A CIP catalogue record for this book is available from the British Library

ISBN 1 84310 726 0

Printed and Bound in Great Britain by
Athenaeum Press, Gateshead, Tyne and Wear

Contents

Acknowledgements

The following individuals have given of their friendship, as well as their kind and unconditional support. Thank you for being good teachers.

Pat Amos, Janiece and Fred Andrews, David Baldner, Beth Barol, Serge Beeler, John and Linda Biever, Clint and Janet Billotte, Joan Berquist, Michael Bomberger, Carly Bonar, Scott, Kim, Alyssa and Alex Bowser, Andrew Boyer, Kathy Brill, Kevin Brownsweiger, Diana Carra-Haugh, Mary Ellen Crawford, Rick Creech, Bill Davis, Lynn Dell, Dan, Sandy and Jason Delecki, Patti Durwachter, Barbara D'Silva, Brian Ellis, Jeff, Tina, Charlie and Esther Franquet, Ginny Focht-New, Gail Gillingham, Kathy Grant, Holly and Michael Hricko, Bill and Eric Jones, Ginny and Sarah Jones, Kathy and Amy Kenevan, Tom, Robin and Melanie Ketchem, Lori Klein, Holly, Jeff and Ben Kofsky, Mary Lapos, Guy Legaré, Bob McAnnaney, Tim and Alison Mekeel, Shane, Patty, and Logan McCoy, Sherry Milchick, Patrick Moore, Barbara Moran, Becky Moyes, Jasmine Lee O'Neill, Looking Glass Consultants, Inc. (Deb Andreas and Lyle Cope), Teri Pentz, John Pfab, Dan Rader, Kim Rhodes, David Rider, Jessica Rivers, Dawn Rudinski, Sharon Salter, Bonnie and Noel Schaefer, Jenn and Kendall Seybert, Shannon and Bonnie Shaull, Stephen Shore, Rae Unger, Michael Vigorito, Tony Yatsko, Ambry Ward, Adam Weber, Matt and Joy Weigand, Sandra Williams.

A special thank you to my publisher, Jessica Kingsley, for being always sensitive, gracious and noble, and for bringing my concept for the cover design to fruition.

Introduction

Whenever I am asked to make a presentation before an audience, I always open with the question "What is autism?" The question is a bit of a set-up because, as one can imagine, the responses are as diverse as the audience, and usually range from "A neurological disorder" to "People who sit and rock all day" to "People who can't communicate and are in their own little world." While none of these perceptions are any less correct than another, they don't best capture the heart of what I wish to share in my role as a humanitarian and teacher. However, once I presented to a large crowd on a university campus. A man named Bob, who has since become my friend, stood up and responded to my question by giving the very best reply of all. He said, "Autism is my son, and my son is beautiful." It is this sentiment that I would like to use in order to set the tone for what follows. For brevity's sake, I will be using the term "autism" to mean all collective autistic spectrum experiences, including autism, Asperger's Syndrome, and Pervasive Developmental Disorder Not Otherwise Specified (PDD NOS). In so doing, I intend no offense or disrespect.

The word "autism" can be so intimidating for those who don't understand it. But let us remember the words of one very young man who said, "I want you to remember that I am no different than you are," meaning we are all more alike than different. I have grown intolerant of reading technical research, diagnosticians' dissertations, and journalist reports that insist upon using terms such as "stricken," "afflicted," and "sufferers" to describe the autistic experience. This is not helpful. Clinically, we know that autism is a neurological difference in brain wiring with no known cause (though theories abound). Autism is neither a contagious disease, nor something that you develop later in life. It is, simply put, part of who you are. While autism can often be perplexing, exasperating, and intriguing for those trying to support a loved one with this experience, there is a great beauty and grace inherent in each individual with autism as well. This is the truth we must always seek lest we become blinded by the "behaviors" that are misunderstood and misinterpreted, causing us to allay our true focus.

My hope for the reader is that I might serve as a guide on a journey toward a greater understanding and heightened awareness of the autistic experience. My wish is to demystify the autistic experience in ways that are concrete and understandable. In so doing, we have the great good fortune to draw upon the wisdom, words and insights of people who can speak to that experience. Our friends graciously provide us with a glimpse through the keyhole into their private world; a world where the rules of the "big world" can't intrude. But to step outside the door is to expose oneself; to surrender one's vulnerability. We are so fortunate to know others who can speak to that balancing act, and describe – quite eloquently – how they accommodate and compensate themselves. To discount, discredit, or invalidate such rich anecdotal information would be unethical. Yet, how closely do we truly listen?

In my work as a consultant, I'm certain that initially I bewilder and disappoint those who are under the impression that my purpose is to "fix" the person. Nothing could be further from the truth. My presence is as an agent of transformation to shift the team's perceptions of the person in a kind and gentle manner. When this occurs truly, the person cannot help but to respond positively to the new ways in which others are demonstrating respect and interacting differently. This is when the seeds of change for all concerned may begin to bud and blossom.

Why, then, are autism "programs" valued so highly? They are myriad, and some even profess to "recover" or "cure" those "afflicted," which is like trying to intentionally alter the color of one's own eyes with tinted lenses. The true color remains: it is only masked. You cannot permanently alter what someone experiences as naturally as his or her eye color, skin color, or heritage. You can, though, in partnership support someone to gently, patiently and lovingly tame, refine, and exert control over one's own experience as much as one is able. Why are there no approaches to supporting individuals predicated entirely upon understanding and learning from the experiences of others? This makes better sense to me and is my impetus for writing this book. Through careful listening, and kind and gentle interactions, our collective invitation *in* awaits us if we allow ourselves to be open to it.

Prologue

It began even before I was born, this connection to *The Wizard of Oz*. As a small child, I used to delight in hearing the story my grandmother would tell about her own brush with *The Wizard of Oz*. It took place shortly after she and my grandfather were newlyweds preparing to move into my grandfather's bachelor apartment, which was on the second floor of a private home. In a June 1999 letter, my grandmother recorded for all time the oft-told story that was always so pleasing to me:

> After we were married in August 1939, we moved into the apartment as our first home. Of course this was the time when *The Wizard of Oz* appeared on the screen. Everyone was whistling and singing the songs. They played on the radio night and day. Whenever the radio played "We're Off to See the Wizard," the young son of the house (who was sixteen or seventeen years old) and I would link arms and skip around the house from room to room, singing. We thought that was great fun, but my new husband didn't appreciate our frivolous display and wouldn't join in! But I still feel like dancing every time I hear the song.

I danced when I heard the song, too. When I was a little boy, my passion was (and remains) *The Wizard of Oz*. Memories of an intense fascination with *The Wizard of Oz* reach back as far as I can recall. I can't explain why it brings me great happiness. I tell people that I didn't pick it — it picked me. And I believe it.

When I was a little boy, math was (and remains) a foreign language. I struggled most with those math problems that necessitated counting small drawings of bundles of pastel-colored dowels in sets. (To me, the bundled dowels were synonymous with the sticks of dynamite in the Roadrunner cartoons.) In retrospect, I suppose the concept was to count by fives, tens, and so on. But I couldn't grasp it.

It is gray and winter, late 1969. I'm seated at a small wooden desk in a classroom of children. It is math test time, and I'm filled with nausea at the prospect. Infinite rows of pleasingly colored pink, green, and blue dowels confront me, intimidating me with their sly and unassuming façade. I try to count the end of each little dowel in each bundle of dynamite with my fingertip. The children around me quickly pace themselves beyond my means. Invariably, I lose count. I start at the beginning, and mark each of those damn dynamite sticks with my pencil point. I attain a new plateau in classroom terror: outright panic. I sweat profusely, my stomach in knots. Ultimately time runs out, and I fail the test.

If only some wise and savvy educator had noticed my struggle and concurrently recognized my passion, I would have welcomed the opportunity to set aside entirely the dowels in favor of counting yellow bricks from the yellow brick road. If my education had been personalized and individualized in this way, my passion could have translated to a multitude of learning opportunities that would have made arithmetic and my whole school career ten times more enjoyable (and likely more successful). I could have been immediately engaged in learning about hot air balloons, breeds of terriers, the pitch and velocity of cyclones, farming and agriculture, magicians and magic, and much more. As such, I contended with a model of conformity that was confusing, overwhelming, and barely tolerable. More about this – and me – later.

Chapter 1

Good Listening

Demystified for the reader in this chapter:

- The importance of focusing our support on the whole person – not just behaviors
- Valuing person-first language
- Acknowledging that aggressive behaviors are the best a person can offer in the moment
- Shattering the stereotype that persons with autism necessarily have mental retardation
- The power of respectful interactions
- Our onus of responsibility for good listening

We know that any approach to supporting someone with autism needs to be as unique and individual as each individual is unique. So often when we speak about autism, we do so in very broad, general terms. And we tend to focus exclusively on behavioral challenges – these are what get our attention most. Nothing convenes a team of people around a meeting room table faster than someone who is hitting, kicking, biting, spitting, cursing, smearing feces, urinating where they shouldn't, destroying property, or doing harm to themselves and others. (We expect compliance but often the ability to discern a function of autism from typical reactive behavior is muddied.)

I was once asked to attend a meeting for my young friend Michael Hricko to determine the need for continuing psychological services. In addition to his parents, the room was full of professionals, including several representatives from Michael's school and the county mental health/mental retardation unit. For two hours, this team of people discussed Michael's "behaviors" which were deemed unmanageable in school; they shifted from reviewing many incidents and topics without any resolve among them. As a guest, I would have made myself very unpopular very quickly had I deliberately interceded to "fix" the situation. (That's not my style anyway; I prefer to sit quietly and interject where appropriate to throw out "bread crumbs," while patiently waiting to see if the team finds them – and what I regard as the true path – on their own.) After a time, I needed to leave the meeting, but just before, one professional team member (perhaps heeding my facial expressions) asked, "Could we talk about some of the *good* things Michael's been doing in school?" As I got up to leave, I leaned over and whispered to this person, "Keep doing what you're doing." In their zealous campaign to vent about the "behaviors," the team had lost sight of the person. And we must always consider the *whole* person in our support.

Once during a presentation, I corrected an audience member's description of someone with autism by tactfully rephrasing their language to reflect person-first language. I would certainly want to be known for all the neat and special things before I'm known first and foremost for the differences that others may perceive as an anomaly. So, rather than saying "autistic boy," we should strive to say, "boy with autism," such that the person (boy) comes before the different way of being (autism).However, a young college special education major challenged my need to make such a public correction. She said she had learned all about person-first language in class but felt there were other things to better focus upon. My response was to wonder how many people with autism she knew with a quality of life equal to her own. The answer is none. That's because of how our society perceives and disrespects people with autism and other different experiences such that they are assigned little value and social standing. Thank goodness self-advocates, parents and professionals are working tirelessly to effect change. But as someone who will be a role model for parents, students and regular education colleagues, it is important that the young woman comprehends why it was necessary to begin with the smallest, most effortless show of respect.

As we will discuss, another great challenge is to learn and understand that aggressive behavior is not necessarily a function of being autistic (or having learning differences, for that matter); nor is it necessarily of that person's volition. We must believe that people have good reasons for doing what they do, and that each is doing the very best that they know how in any given moment. If there were another way – a kinder, gentler, better way – that would surely be the first option of choice for the person with autism. But so often what someone knows how to do has been learned, proven effective (i.e. it usually "works" despite negative repercussions), or is so engrained that it is the path of least resistance, even though it may further perpetuate undue stereotypes.

Must we subscribe to one all-encompassing method of supporting the person with autism, or can there be an eclectic mix of formal and informal supports wherein the person guides us to what works, what is comfortable, and what makes sense? (One parent dubbed this the "stew" approach; that is, taking the best of what makes sense from the available supports, given what she knows to be true about her child.) We can draw upon others' experiences in tailoring support that promotes acceptance, confidence, and tenderness. How closely do we truly listen to what people are telling us – not just in speech, but also through other means of communication?

Ultimately, labels are unimportant. Regardless of what causes autism, or how we choose to define it, it's how we interact with someone that is most important. We should approach our friends with autism in a manner that demonstrates respect: presume intellect always. The paradigm shift in the field of autism shatters the stereotype that autism necessarily co-occurs with mental retardation. Although approximately seventy-five percent of persons with autism have a label of mental retardation, this is not always the case. The autistic experience can be considered as you would the differences in a person with cerebral palsy: the physical body presents with challenges that do not necessarily impair one's intellect.

One of the greatest mistakes we can make is to talk about someone in front of them as if they are not there (often in disparaging, disrespectful terms). We do this constantly and absent-mindedly, even when we deny that we do it at all.

Parents and professionals have sworn to me that they do not behave like this, and then, in the next breath, turn around and do it – with the person sitting right beside them! Is it no wonder, then, that the person in question proceeds to cover their ears and rock to avert the hurtful words (thus perpetuating stereotypical behavior which others point to as an example, "See!")? This happens all the time such that it has become an unconscious habit for too many parents and professionals.

The three most powerful words any of us can say about ourselves are "I was wrong." If you know that you do this "thing," it is important that you immediately refrain and desist from it, and approach the offended individual to offer your sincere apology. If you seek to be absolved through honest confession of your ignorance, you will be forgiven. There is no shame in making this admission, only growth and liberation. People with autism are innately gentle beings, and are oftentimes remarkably forgiving. I can state this with conviction because I have received many personal testimonies, phone calls, letters and e-mail communications from people who have swallowed their pride in this manner, and, afterwards, have contacted me to tell me of the extraordinary, near-miraculous changes that began to occur in their relationship as a result of their honest confession and pledge of respect. The mother of my friend Clint Billotte did this very thing, and was witness to immediate changes in their camaraderie and growth in Clint's communication. She has at long last begun to connect with the person she always knew was "inside" him. The son of another friend became more verbally fluent, whereas previously he was largely silent. Still another mother shared that after her confession, her son sat back and soundly applauded her as if to indicate, "Yeah! Mom finally gets it!"

Even positive, glowing comments made about someone in front of others and without their permission can also be perceived as embarrassing or disingenuous. (How many of us have felt a certain prickly humiliation courtesy of well-intentioned colleagues who surprised us by singing "Happy Birthday" publicly?) Please don't praise every movement or eye gaze a person makes, because you are creating further stigma by giving undue attention not given to peers for the same gestures. The novelty of your saying "Good sitting," "Good eating," (or any other statement that begins with the overused word "good") quickly wears thin and smacks of insincerity. Many people with autism have social limitations but a keen sensitivity for disingenuous interactions. Request permission to share information, weigh your words carefully and be selective when giving praise.

Let's also be very mindful of the responsibilities and expectations we assign to parents and family members. People have busy lives, complex and complicated lives. Sometimes supporting the person with an autistic experience simply doesn't take priority within each family at any given time. Oftentimes, professionals become quite frustrated because a family isn't following a support plan; isn't documenting behaviors; or isn't marking off a reinforcement chart. We should start with what works for the person and family presently, and be mindful of what we're imposing that's new and different. Parents have told me that their single greatest resource is not therapy, aides, or programming but being able to talk with another parent in a similar situation. And know, too, that it is parents who are in the best position to provide important information about their loved one, and, as such, are extremely valuable members of an individual's team.

We also need to practice better listening. So often, people with autism are providing us clear communication; we just aren't paying attention closely enough. Listening, of course, means being open and taking in everything about us. The communication expressed by the very gentle is often simple, benign and understated. We should take the empathy, the kindness, the compassion, the patience, and the sensitivity we think we have now for supporting someone with autism, and double it. It is that minute and tight a concentric circle in which some people exist. Meet them there, and we might come close to what someone with autism could hope to expect from us. And if they can't hope to expect it from those who profess to care the most, whom, then, can they hope to expect it from? The big world certainly doesn't accommodate for individual needs and sensitivities; everyone needs a place where they can feel safe, comfortable, loved and understood. In order to move forward, we need to subscribe to the notion that our interactions with others must occur as intellectual partners. If you do this sincerely, you will be invited in. To do otherwise is to risk inducing damage and distrust in our relationships. Fully embracing respect in our interactions with someone with autism is the single most important thing we can ever do.

Guiding Principles – Good Listening

- We are all more alike than different

- Embrace supporting the whole person

- Using person-first language models respect

- People have good reasons for doing what they do, and are doing the very best they know how in the moment

- Presume intellect

- Parents are partners

- Demonstrate respect by not talking about someone in their presence especially in disrespectful or disingenuous ways

- Seek forgiveness by apologizing for previous slights and offenses

- Pledge to double your show of empathy, kindness, compassion, patience and sensitivity

Chapter 2

Liberation Through Communication

Demystified for the reader in this chapter:

- The critical importance of self-expression through effective, reliable, and understandable communication
- Understanding that we erroneously equate verbal communication with intellect
- Why making eye contact in conversation is difficult
- The challenges of navigating everyday social conversation
- Valuing "movie talk" in social conversation
- The importance of offering viable alternatives to verbal communication
- Deconstructing communications that transpire "for no apparent reason"
- How to demonstrate safety and trust with communication partners

We communicate in many ways: facial expressions, silence, body language and gestures, written words, music and art, e-mail, actions, icons, communication devices and sign language to name a few. Every day we support people in expressing their wants, needs, desires, opinions, passions, thoughts, and ideas. Self-expression is critical in the choices people make about living their lives, in explaining emotion, in reporting pain, in describing side effects of medication, or in giving consent. However, above all, we place a high value on our ability to communicate through speech, though verbal communication accounts for just about seven percent of all our communication, according to a 2001 *USA Today* poll. When we think about the clinical definitions of autism spectrum experiences, we most often think about people with communication challenges, which, in turn, lead to challenges in social interactions. People who interact with us verbally may be seen as having greater intellect, and stronger social skills. If someone doesn't speak, we are wont to make assumptions about their intellect. This is a stereotype to shatter.

Concurrent with valuing verbal communication, we also highly value one's ability to maintain eye contact in conversation. Just like the assumptions we may make about someone who doesn't talk, we may think that the person who can't look us in the eye is being rude, has something to hide, or is dishonest. When those with an autistic experience have difficulty doing this consistently, we have been trained to physically, intrusively tilt their chins toward us and implore "Look at me," overlooking that, in certain cultures, not making eye contact is a show of respect. Most significant to recognize, however, is how astoundingly disrespectful we've been in taking the liberty of grasping someone's flesh with our fingers in a very tactile-defensive area and without permission. If the same person grabbed back in the same intrusive manner – suddenly and without warning – their actions would be quickly categorized as "physical aggression," and would be addressed through behavior management.

My friend Barbara Moran states: "If you *look* at someone, you're too busy (i.e. visually distracted) to listen!" She's right, of course. Many people with autism are extremely visual. Attempting to maintain eye contact with someone in conversation can be a frustrating exercise in futility if you are distracted by the person's mouth, teeth, tongue, saliva, skin imperfections, receding hairline, dangling jewelry, flecks of hue in their eyes, reflections on glasses, and much more. I can very nearly guarantee that the person who is not giving direct eye contact, and appears not to be listening is listening more closely than the person who is compelled to make direct eye contact. Barbara has learned to adapt to others' expectations by staring at someone's ear lobe, sustaining the illusion of making eye contact.

I always advocate that the very best time to put effort into making direct eye contact is upon being introduced to someone. (This means, though, being so visually absorbed that many of us will forget the person's name or what they've said.) After this initial "connection," lack of direct eye contact may be perceived as less suspicious. Consider carefully those times when direct eye contact is absolutely warranted for the person you know and care about, explain why it behooves the person in the moment, and make it meaningful and attractive to do so. I have also discovered that many folks with autism don't understand what an introductory handshake "communicates" such that this initial connection is rather flat. As a child, my father drilled me in reciprocating a firm, confident handshake as an alternative to what he called "a dead fish." Explaining the importance of first impressions in conjunction with a discussion about direct eye contact, a solid – but not overwhelming – handshake and private practice should be helpful.

Many folks with autism are without verbal speech, or have limited vocal capabilities. It is unacceptable to accept that just because someone doesn't talk, that's "just the way they are." It is incumbent upon those of us who know and care about someone with autism to determine viable, under-standable and reliable means of communication that make sense for that person, including at least one method of communication that is immediately accessible by that person at all times, day or night. (For who among us would want someone regulating the use of our voice?) We simply cannot rest until we figure this out, for people are waiting patiently in silence for us to do so. I grieve for the tens of thousands of people who have lived and died in silence, and who were possessed of brilliant minds.

Rick Creech is a friend with cerebral palsy. Rick does not speak. He uses a wheelchair, and needs support in eating, bathing, and using the bathroom. Rick knows what it is for people to judge by what they see. What people don't see at first glance is Rick's sense of humor and his unique take on life, documented in his autobiographical manuscript, *Reflections from a Unicorn*. Rick dubbed himself with the nickname "unicorn" because he wears a metal band around his forehead from which extends a long silver rod. Rick has enough control of his head and neck muscles to use the rod to touch the keypad of a communication device that is mounted to the front of his wheelchair.

Rick accepts that he is dependent upon others, but created a situation in which he determines how much he is going to depend on someone, and where that dependency ends. In his manuscript, Rick speaks to communication issues:

> I am a unique person. Although having cerebral palsy makes me different in some ways from other people, the state of being different does not make me a unique person. Being unable to articulate words and produce oral speech does not make me a unique person. Everyone has the danger of losing the ability of speech. Having limitations does not make a person unique. In spite of not having oral speech, I developed good linguistic skills, and I learned to use augmented communication, becoming a good communicator.
>
> The usual reaction to communicating with a speech-impaired person is nervous anxiety. Some people cannot overcome their fear of the disability and are never able to interact with the person within. The speech-impaired person cannot interact with these people because they run from the augmented speaker. They avoid eye contact, mumble, shift weight from one foot to another, and show every sign of wanting to flee. In this case, the person with the handicap is not the one who uses an augmented speaking device. The handicapped person is the one who cannot communicate.

Through the use of assistive technology, Rick's good and great thinking is liberated, and we can appreciate his ability to ably work full time in the education system, and be a great husband and father.

Navigating everyday conversation woven with sarcasm, innuendo, and double entendre is difficult for most people with autism because so many others are privy to a covert social code, being an inherent, learned understanding of the hidden meanings embedded in our language. (Those of us who are slow to catch on are often labeled "gullible" or "naive.") You may recall the old Marx Brothers movie in which Groucho and his brothers are greeted at a mansion's front door by a butler who invites them to "walk this way." The butler proceeds off screen, striding with an eccentric jaunt. The visual joke is that the Marx Brothers goosestep after him in the same, exaggerated manner because they have interpreted the butler's words literally. It's a joke as old as vaudeville, and such miscommunications and misunderstandings in language are the hallmarks of what many people consider comedic. (Aren't Shakespeare's best known comedies all predicated upon miscommunications?) I don't watch a lot of television but the commercials I've seen for the program *Third Rock from the Sun* lead me to believe that the show's characters are autistic because they interpret "earthling" communications literally (hence the comedy, once again).

The book *Alice in Wonderland* makes for an interesting reverse analogy of the contention that many folks with autism describe themselves as feeling like aliens trying to assimilate among humans. Alice is the "normal" one trying to fit in amongst others with very different ways of being, very unusual ways of thinking, and who are possessed of a logic that works for them, but who continually perplex and frustrate her. Interesting still is that the characters whom Alice meets are oftentimes confrontational, harsh and abrasive, and have little patience with her. In one episode, there is a debate around the table at the tea party between Alice, the March Hare, and the Mad Hatter. The March Hare implores Alice to "say what you mean." Alice responds, "I do...at least I mean what I say – that's the same thing you know." But is it?

Consider the story of the mother so pleased with her son's interactions at the bakery concerning the ingredients for his birthday cake until the baker asked, "What would you like your cake to say?" To which the boy replied, "Are you crazy? Cakes don't talk!" As in the film *A is for Autism*, there is an exquisite concreteness that draws a gentleman with autism to prize a Shell Oil tin simply because the word "shell" is written on the shell logo – it says exactly what it means, and can never mean or say anything other than what it is. Oftentimes, people with autism are as clear, direct and concise in their communicative expressions. They say what they mean, and mean what they say. That is, "no" means no – definitively. Nothing will cause someone's frustration level to escalate faster in conversation than your not accepting "no" for an answer and pressing someone to recant or reconsider his or her statement. One may also feel similarly if you repeat the question until you get the answer you want; rephrase the question multiple ways; or solicit others to intervene (so the that person is besieged in stereo). This is not helpful or respectful.

Some folks who are verbose and offer too much information need support in understanding that some social interactions are like ordering from a menu; you don't tell the waitress your life story, you just tell her enough information to get you what you want. Videotaping (always with the knowledge and permission of the person) may be useful if it is reviewed with the person in a gentle, respectful, and private manner. I am cautioning here because it is quite traumatic for any of us to see and hear ourselves on video, let alone those of us who are exquisitely sensitive beings. However, as is true of us all, we don't see ourselves as others see us, such that watching ourselves can be a very sobering experience. One young man of high school age was often loud and silly in class, monopolizing his peer's conversations until he viewed a videotape of a small workgroup in which he participated. He wasn't quite the handsome and brilliant classroom raconteur he imagined himself to be. After going into a "shutdown" mode for about twenty-four hours, he emerged more reserved. He now understood how best to tame and refine himself in order to better assimilate and meet the circumstantial expectations.

It may also be useful to have a "scripted" sense of what to say in advance of some social situations that require awkward or uncomfortable interaction. Many young people with milder forms of autism or Asperger's Syndrome already do this independently; it just hasn't been acknowledged as acceptable. Some are brilliant actors and adept mimics. They routinely extract lines of dialogue from favorite films, cartoons, commercials, TV shows and videos and repeat them in socially appropriate ways. (It has become quite easy to do this, especially in the video age where the same show or movie can be viewed repeatedly at will.) Often, the dialogue is spoken with the exact emotion and inflection as the actor's voice, and referred to by parents as "TV talk," or "movie talk."

Children with autism who use movie talk become so adept at doing it that it often goes undetected by others (except constant caregivers or stay-at-home moms who are in a position to overhear the repetitious playback). One mother of a girl with Asperger's told me of her daughter's fondness for Disney's *Little Mermaid* movie. Her husband came home one evening and scolded the girl about something, and her daughter responded by exclaiming, "Father, no!" which was delivered with the same diction as Ariel the mermaid uttered it. Dad shrugged it off, thinking nothing of it, but mom, listening from the kitchen, immediately recognized the dialogue.

This phenomenon is not relegated to kids with autism, and is, in fact, appropriate of typically developing peers. You may recall a TV commercial from several years ago that comically explored this, dubbing the movie talk, "narratum verbatim." It involved two young children who mimicked the line from a video, "What's up, little pup?" with disturbing frequency. Its humor was derived of a universal experience shared by many parents. Adults do this all the time too. How many people recognize the humor and familiarity in certain catch phrases used in everyday conversation, such as *Who Wants to Be a Millionare*'s "Is that your final answer?" or Clint Eastwood's "Go ahead, make my day!" It is all acceptable when "typical" children and adults do it. Why, then, is it something to raise concern or to extinguish completely when others do it?

We should acknowledge movie talk as a strength. It is communication that has developed as an independently discovered coping strategy that can be built upon, not torn down and discarded. Kids who use movie talk effectively understand the expectation that they "pass," fit in, and get by such that they strive to assimilate seamlessly. Some are more successful than others, but I can think of no finer tool for feeling a modicum of confidence in entering social situations full of uncertainty.

Practical, formalized application of movie talk should begin with identifying its origins. (The constant caregiver or stay-at-home mom will be in the best position to do this.) Identify the favorite film, cartoon or TV show. Are there preferential trends, a particular episode or scene that holds the most appeal? Next, consider the person's favorite character. What's the identification connection? Concurrently identify specific lines of dialogue, emotion, meaning and intent while also considering the character's accompanying body language. Discuss future settings and situations in which it may be okay to effectively "put it back out."

Next, identify the favorite character's colleagues. Who's good and decent, and who's not so nice? Now, who in real life is most like them? Reflect upon real life situations that parallel the movie situations as best you can.

Lay a collaborative foundation by forming a partnership with the person with autism. Are you an ally in the person's life who can do this? Use a superhero analogy to explain that there are occasions when a few select people in his or her life know the superhero's identity, but that most people remain unaware. Using movie talk, and assuming bits of a character's voice tone, inflection, and body language is like that. Acknowledge when and where in the past movie talk was already used. Explore what made it work or why it didn't work. Also discuss ways of keeping it all as subtle and discreet as possible. The purpose will be defeated by obvious affects that appear overdone and clichéd.

Develop a "working" written catalog from which to draw. Categorize it by emotions best suited for situations. Of course, unpredictable reactions and response will always arise in real life situations, but the person will be much better equipped in such situations than before. Finally, spend time rehearsing, first as the movie characters in scene reenactments and then as yourselves, adjusting the circumstances to reflect real life situations. Explore differences and variations from exact dialogue, which will promote someone's ability to be flexible in the moment (i.e. able to adapt by thinking quickly). Cautious and discreet use of video playback of your rehearsals may also be considered as a learning tool. The greatest emphasis in exploring the concept of movie talk is to communicate that one does not become the character; rather one seeks to embrace their best traits, body language, and dialogue in subtle, socially acceptable ways.

Beyond this, I also recommend encouraging participation in legitimate acting opportunities through local community theatre or school dramatic productions. Many people with autism or Asperger's have found solace and a positive outlet through acting. Becoming another character holds great appeal – especially if you have damaged self-esteem – in that you get to become someone other than yourself temporarily. There is opportunity to learn about the reciprocity of social interactions in a non-threatening manner because everything is already scripted for you (i.e.

you never say the "wrong" thing). Acting also offers the opportunity to learn more about "reading" body language and facial expressions in a controlled, objective context for those who are challenged by such details. There's an additional social component through rehearsing and interacting with fellow thespians. Often people interested in theatre are very open and accepting of others' differences. Self-validation is acknowledged through giving a laudable performance, and eliciting accolades from peers and audience members.

People that I speak with about movie talk usually share the same reservations. What if the person seems to identify with evil or violent characters? Or, what about inappropriate use of language? Let's acknowledge that most of what is presented on TV and in movies represents exaggerated, controversial human behavior. Many of us would never dream of doing and saying a lot of what these characters do and say because we understand the potential consequences. We'd offend and alienate friends, neighbors, and family; we'd break laws; we'd be victimized; or we'd get fired from our jobs. That's why it's called entertainment; we're safe at home in front of our television sets watching (and rooting for) characters that behave in ways we'd never dare reenact. Again we confront the covert social code. Many of us understand such consequences for behavior, but they may need to be taught and explained to others. This is why, very often, young men with Asperger's find themselves at the center of grave concern because they've communicated a sexually provocative sentiment or action that was not well received (though in the TV show or movie, the guy who gets the girl said or did the same thing – it worked then). They are not sex perverts or menaces. Once someone steps back from the situation to investigate objectively – and I've had police officers confirm this – they will usually discover that movie talk was involved, having been expressed with abject honesty, sincerity, and best intentions. While preventable through private intervention, what transpired is that the movie talk backfired in real life.

Carol Gray's (1994) social stories also make enormous good sense in visually supporting people to quell anxiety and understand what is expected and what to expect of certain situations through simple picture stories and/or written statements, age appropriately tailored; this concept is cousin to movie talk.

Similar to exploring movie talk and acting, I also recommend pursuing music as a means of communication, especially for folks unable to speak. We know that music is very important for most folks with autism. All of music is scripted as well, and I have known people who didn't speak but could sing, or whose speech was discernible through song. Some possess a natural proclivity for understanding how music "works," and are able to facilely weave in and out of complex melodies and harmonies. Classical music, in particular, is of such divine composition that it is often a tremendous aid in supporting one's concentration and soothing of mood. Using song to communicate what is to be learned is as old as parenting.

In music there is what's referred to as "call" and "response." There is a time when, according to the scripted composition, you sing or play your part on an instrument (call) and there's a time to remain silent and await the response from communication partners. In this way, reciprocation of communication in conversation may be likened to a successful musical interaction. An adept music therapist understands and employs these concepts in their work by building upon the verbalizations or musical sounds offered by the person with autism. The music therapist can be a resource in generalizing such approaches across a person's environments and embedded within the flow of his or her typical daily routines outside the therapy sessions. Remember, the emphasis is on reciprocal interaction and output of communication. With music as the language, the outcomes may include focus, control, discipline and – above all else – fun!

If someone is making verbalizations – even if it's echolalia – go with it. This is someone who is working hard at trying to fit in by doing what is expected of him or her. Acknowledge it as communication! Validate and encourage the communication by responding to it, even if it's to be honest in stating, "I don't understand everything you're saying, but it sounds beautiful and I love to hear you talk." But do not simply placate someone by responding as if you understand them if you truly do not; this will only fuel everyone's frustration. Instead, ask clarifying questions or suggest the person show you what they want, if possible. Bring in a strong speech-language pathologist who can offer opportunities for everyone who interacts with the individual to naturally build upon that person's speech within the flow of his or her typical daily routines, and in discussion of topics attractive and appealing for that person.

For those without verbal speech or with limited speech, consider other forms of alternative communication. In bearing the philosophy that the person will guide us to what works for them, I support a total communication approach by providing the individual with the luxury of sifting through the options, casting off what doesn't work, and retaining what makes good sense for them. Do not be so quick to discard one communication method; remember that this is a learning time for everyone, and adapting to change is challenging for many people with autism.

I caution folks about actively pursuing sign language because it is not universally understood across all environments. The person who has been taught sign language cannot enter the local McDonald's with the expectation that the person at the counter will understand the order being placed; regrettably, it just doesn't happen. Even within the deaf community, there are splintered factions that use modified variations of sign language. If an adult with autism living in a community residential setting is taught sign language, his or her staff must also learn it and become as fluent. The great caveat lies in maintaining consistency despite staff turnover. If a child has learned some basic signs within the context of the family unit, then I would encourage maintaining those signs within the family because they are useful, purposeful and understood. But I am then equally encouraging of introducing a range of alternative communication options to maximize the potential for full community participation.

Assistive technology can include computers and computer programs as well as a great variety of compact, portable devices with keyboards that display letters, pictures, icons or words, and voice output. Many such devices are small and discreet, and can be used publicly without attracting much attention to oneself. The ability to independently access assistive technology can be facilitated with adaptive equipment, such as the wand used by my friend Rick Creech, or an infrared laser device like that worn around my friend John Pfab's head which enables him to direct the beam to activate his keyboard without physically touching it. Many school systems, special educators and speech-language professionals are familiar with such devices and will know how to arrange an assessment or a trial loan.

Picture Exchange Communication Systems (PECS) are helpful, particularly with very young children just learning to express their needs in ways that are acceptable and honored (without a lot of guesswork by other parties). PECS involves an individual communicating their wants and needs through giving their communication partner a small image, icon or word imprinted on a card. PECS may be used to support and elicit speech output by requesting the giver concurrently to verbally identify the picture to the receiver. It's a concept that makes good sense, particularly given the very visual, concrete nature of many people with autism. In my opinion, though, PECS should not be exclusive of other communication options because PECS are limited to the parameters that we set around what *we think* someone wants to communicate to us. PECS are therefore not boundless in promoting someone's free expression of their limitless thoughts and feelings.

Facilitated Communication (FC) is a process predicated upon trusting relationships. The person with autism (or someone with the inability to communicate in ways that are universally understood) allows themselves to be physically supported by their facilitator in order to gain the muscle coordination and motor-planning control necessary to indicate a want, need or thought by touching a keyboard, letterboard, pictures or icons. Many people use FC best if they are physically supported by the facilitator under their hand and fingers, at the wrist, under their elbow, or by touching their shoulder. The person who is physically supported may require less or more support depending upon the comfort level in the relationship with the facilitator or the environment, and such support will be gradually faded as the person gains confidence. Years after its introduction in the USA in the 1990s, FC remains a hotly contested, controversial and debatable communication method because of the potential for the facilitator to knowingly or unknowingly author communication unintended by the person being facilitated. However, with independence from facilitator support as the goal, it is one of few available communication methods that is boundless. Teams wishing to explore FC should do so in a thoughtful, fair and rational manner through balanced research, and may wish to compose their own mutually agreed upon guidelines of informed exploration.

My good and kind friend, Jenn Seybert, is a self-advocate who is passionate about the freeing liberation Facilitated Communication can offer:

> I am so happy to be able to communicate and let my thoughts known, whether I am happy, sad, angry, frustrated or horrified. It was raging frustration all the years I was silent. My behavior showed it. Life is very different. I don't carry that frustration with me anymore. I have my moments, but not weeks of bad times.

In addition to autism, Jenn presently has a label of learning difference. In her role as a self-advocate and founder of a Pennsylvania-based group of FC users, The Lonesome Doves, she has been brutally honest in stating that, prior to FC, her behavior was appalling and stereotypical. She is now a successful college student.

My beloved friend Michael expresses sentiments similar to Jenn through his use of FC:

> First, I am not free. I write my thoughts only it does not free me. I am still a prisoner in myself. I will know true freedom when I can type on my own. Please understand to communicate is what I want to do and it has changed my life... It is an opening to another wonderful world. It is a pathway to enlightenment. It is liberating in that way as well for others... For me, to say what I think is a release like no other... I am smart but I don't look it, and people judge by what they see, not who I am... My typing is my voice. It is loud and strong. People will listen and learn and help me when they hear it. Only now do they help, truly help. Before it was about what they *thought* I needed, never what I needed... Without communication only alone are we... It makes you a person in other people's eyes.

Offering new and different communication options is, in essence, a seduction. This is because what we are offering must be powerful enough to supersede whatever it is that person does presently to get them what they want. For example, there is no motivation for someone to exchange a picture card – or sign the word – for juice if they presently go to the refrigerator and point, take someone to what they want, or pour a glass of juice for themselves. There are other communications that take priority over this. Similarly, encouraging the communication "please help" in the form of a picture card, a sign, or a voice output is not helpful at all. "Please help" may be a very broad and vague concept for an individual, and could have a thousand interpretations. Such a communication needs to be more concretely delineated and defined. We are not allowing for personal growth if someone is merely accommodating our expectations in providing us with the "correct" or appropriate response to what we are eliciting. Compliance for the sake of compliance does not equal success. We must think beyond the typical and ordinary to truly have impact.

We know that disruptive behavior is most often a form of communicating something that otherwise cannot be communicated explicitly and succinctly. One friend with autism described the incommunicable emotions she once experienced:

> Autistic people get big rages. I throw tantrums. I have waves of rage that come surging. I need to feel safe and always in control of my life, my world. It gets drowned in frustration and anger. I do wish the anger would go away. All emotions hurt... And I can't stand anything unpredictable. Crying is my way to show emotion. If I'm a lot happy or frustrated or angry or sleepy or afraid, I cry. Emotions hurt me. They are all too much.

This person's self-expression contains two very salient observations that will become significant, overarching themes throughout our support of those with an autistic experience. Mark these words carefully: "I need to feel safe and always in control," and "I can't stand anything unpredictable."

We often hear others' behaviors qualified with the phrase "for no apparent reason." There may be times when expressed emotions are indeed quite appropriate, just exaggerated. Consider the child who wants so desperately to be held but for whom close human contact is overwhelming. The expectation may be that the child "gives mommy a kiss." While the child may truly want to kiss mommy, it is all too much and the kiss becomes a bite. And the bite begets itself. The child is labeled a "biter," and there is an urgency to "fix" the behavior rather than understand its meaning.

Barbara Moran tells the story of being on a school van that bounced over a pothole in the road. The boy behind her remarked that he felt as though his stomach was left somewhere down the street. Because Barbara is an artist, she immediately got a visual picture of the boy's disemboweled stomach flip-flopping in the road. This was amusing, and she laughed. Then, because everyone on the van experienced the same sensation in the same moment, she imagined everyone's stomach flip-flopping in the road – and she laughed harder. And she laughed uncontrollably. Her mind pictures were unbeknownst to anyone else, and because she was laughing "for no apparent reason" she was severely reprimanded.

We are also quick to assume disinterest, avoidance, or incompetence when someone doesn't respond to a request immediately. We have been conditioned to become uncomfortable when this occurs. A computer screen checklist may pop up in our mind, and we scan through the range of possible explanations as to precisely why someone is not responding to our communication. Did they not hear me? Did they not understand? Are they deaf, or don't speak my language? Does my breath smell? Have I offended them? Allowing the opportunity for someone to process what is being asked is a luxury for us, and an exercise in control and concentration for others. It is helpful to simply stand and wait, perhaps silently counting. Allowing for such wait time may be a tedious exercise for us, but a necessary one. How reasonable is it to expect someone to act on our command when that person is struggling to assimilate all the stimuli that are bombarding him or her? We expect it because few of us know what it is to feel our senses assaulted, or to be unable to make an immediate brain–body connection. My experience has shown that allowing for such process time is usually successful.

We expect instantaneous trust and safety in the way that we blindly trust that the car coming toward us won't cross the double yellow line and collide with our vehicle; that the chef who has prepared our food hasn't laced it with strychnine; or that the person cutting our hair will cut it reasonably within the parameters that we've set for them. We know, too, that there is a predictable sameness in our daily routines and activities. For example, we have a trust in the safety of knowing that when we leave our home, we'll find a familiar destination the same way we usually do; we'll park our car and enter an establishment as always; and upon leaving, we'll be able to find our way from the building and to our car as before; and that the same key that turned off the car's ignition, will also start it again. Factor out some or all of the elements from this sequence, and anxiety, frustration, panic and chaos reign for any one of us. We must earn trust in interacting with someone with autism who doesn't have a solid grasp of these concepts such that they are new and novel with each occasion.

Building the foundation for trust to flourish in the context of a relationship means first making yourself "real" to the person with the autistic experience. Similar to understanding the concept of blind trust in what is or isn't most likely to transpire in our everyday lives, we too have a lot of information about the person we know and care about which we take for granted. We know intimate details about his or her personal habits, their medical and psychiatric history, their history of living arrangements, their idiosyncrasies, present and prior offenses, their current medications, and their Intelligence Quotient (IQ). That person knows nothing about us, such that we are likely to join the long parade of two-dimensional cardboard cutouts that have drifted in and out of that person's life without consequence or connection. If you are genuine and sincere in your desire to establish trust, you need to make yourself real, whole and three-dimensional such that the individual has an incentive to become personally invested in you as a human being. This means providing the person (well in advance of your first meeting, if possible) with a clear photograph of yourself and written information about who you are such as your full name, your birth date, your hobbies, favorite colors, favorite music, pets, loved ones, how you spend your time – anything at all with which you are comfortable revealing. The information you've shared may then be the basis of your first conversation with the person. In so doing, the unbalanced scales of the relationship become evenly tipped, and we may begin to build the foundation for mutual respect and open communication in a fair manner.

Providing someone with the support to communicate openly and freely also means risking our disapproval with what they are telling us. The people receiving our support may not have had the privilege of growing, learning, and understanding about life, relationships, and social concepts in the same way that many of us have. As a result, we may not be able to fully support the choices someone is making. That's the dignity of independence. Caregivers are forever tempering a balance around personal and informed choice; health, safety and welfare issues; and compromise. It is a challenge that should be personalized and individualized to each unique circumstance. It also means respecting reasonable risk.

The ability for people with autism to communicate openly and freely is at the very heart of our work as caregivers, supporters and advocates. Please spend time considering the ways in which you can further explore communication opportunities for the people that you know, support and care about. What are some of the ways in which you can build upon individual strengths, passions, and interests in providing for meaningful interactions? What are some technical supports and local resources that could be pursued? How can you build upon the ways in which someone presently communicates? Please use what others are telling us about the ways they communicate as a foundation toward building and enhancing communication.

Guiding Principles – Liberation Through Communication

- Being unable to communicate verbally is not an indicator of intellect

- Demonstrate respect by never physically moving someone's face to compel eye contact

- When eye contact is warranted, explain why and make it appealing to do so

- It is unacceptable to accept that just because someone doesn't talk, that's "just the way they are"

- We cannot rest until we enable someone to access an effective, reliable, and understandable means of communication that is immediately and independently accessible for that person at all times

- Support the person in "cracking" the covert social code

- Be mindful of our language: say what you mean, and mean what you say

- Acknowledge the value of movie talk as an independently discovered coping mechanism, and make practical use of it

- Offer a wide range of communication alternatives; the person will guide us to what works best

- Whatever you offer that is new and different must be so powerful that it supersedes whatever the person does now to get them what they want

- "Disruptive" behavior is communication of something that cannot be expressed in any other way in the moment

- Assure that the person's communication is not merely placating our expectations

- People with autism need to feel control over that which is unpredictable

- In order to elicit the safety and trust of a communication partner, you must first make yourself "real"

Chapter 3

Valuing Passions

Demystified for the reader in this chapter:

- Distinguishing that personal passions are not obsessions or compulsions
- Why it is crucial that passions must not be "earned" or extinguished
- Building upon passions as a bridge to social interactions, learning, avocations and vocations
- Cautions in the misinterpretation of passions

I've already shared some information about my life's passion. Think on the passion(s) of the person with autism that you care most about, and consider how to build on those passions to create communication and learning opportunities that are meaningful and interesting to that person. Everyone has a passion. (No, a passion is not flicking a light switch on and off. Such an activity is deciphered in the next chapter.) People with autism are no different, and each person has at least one topic or subject area about which they are absolutely passionate. For some it is locomotives, dinosaurs, airplanes, astronomy, or insects, to name a few. In addition to *The Wizard of Oz*, sub-categories of my childhood passions included gargoyles on cathedrals and churches, Greek mythology and the Loch Ness Monster.

Sometimes people tell me that the person they support has no passion. They do indeed. They may just be unable to communicate or express it, or it may be intensely private and personal; something they are unable (or unwilling) to share because it is all they have, and they can't risk revealing something that makes them feel safe and comfortable. Too much of what enables people to feel safe and comfortable is chipped away by others. Yet all our professional, formal plans of documentation request this information in one form or another.

People who know me are aware that I'm passionate about using passions as a means of engaging others. I was validated when, in 1996, I heard Temple Grandin speak about a similar concept. She advocated building on interests with an eye toward future employment. Temple has written about her childhood fixation (I prefer the word "passion" because it's non-clinical sounding) for automatic sliding doors, and how that could be used as inspiration for further education, such as locating the door manufacturing company on a map and measuring the miles from it to the person's residence or school. Such "crosswalking" of the concept incorporates math and geography with the passion.

My dear friend Jasmine Lee O'Neill, author of *Through the Eyes of Aliens*, has followed this path too in encouraging strong interests and creating pleasing environmental memories. Some might react to the intensity of such interests by labeling them as perseverative or restricted. Indeed, the

Diagnostic and Statistical Manual uses such language in establishing criteria of concern. However, proactive opportunity lies patiently awaiting discovery, as my good friend Bonnie Schaefer came to understand.

Bonnie's nine-year-old son Noel had been struggling with a typical classroom curriculum until Bonnie integrated his passions into his lessons. Instead of pressing him to practice handwriting, which was difficult for Noel, she simply asked him if he could write out a list of his favorite computer programs, which he did eagerly. In fact, Bonnie has set aside an emphasis on handwriting altogether in favor of typing. Noel's history lessons became fascinating for him when he began learning about ancient Greece and Rome, which he saw as a chance to go back in time and connect with the scientists, philosophers and artists with whom he could best relate. From this also came an appreciation for the Latin root of words common in many languages, such that a guessing game ensued. Learning the names of Greek and Roman gods crosswalked to learning the names of planets (many of which are named after Roman gods), which Noel drew on paper in order and with great enthusiasm. Noel's love of history also applied to the study of the painting techniques of famous artists in art class, which he then imitated in drawings of subjects of his own choosing. In language arts, Noel writes freely about his passions within curricular parameters. As Noel grows, the potential to translate his passions to other areas of learning is limitless.

We must be mindful, then, of the casual use of the clinical terms "obsession" or "compulsion" to describe someone's intensely passionate interest (these terms are further explored in the next chapter). Now that we can better appreciate the value of passions, it is crucial that we do not use the person's passion as a reward that must be earned or strived for like a dangling carrot. Think about your weakest skill – the task or subject area you least liked, and least excelled in during school. Now think of having to concentrate, attend and focus upon that weakest skill such that you must produce something of acceptable quality in order to earn your passion. For many of us, our passion may not be a thing but a person. As part of a presentation I make to demystify the autistic experience, I require the audience to draw a snowman at my brisk, specific, out-of-sequence direction – and on top of their heads, without peeking. It is often described as a frustrating, difficult exercise because of attempting to assimilate information, process it differently from what is accustomed, and trying to produce a product of quality in order to "please" the instructor. Very rarely is anyone able to experience any modicum of success. However, the analogy I provide is consolation that – while individual passions weren't earned due to poor work quality – we will practice drawing a snowman on top of our heads every day until we get it right and have finally achieved the chance to indulge in what pleases and comforts us most. With facetious observation, I comment that it may take days, weeks or months, depending on the individual, but I zealously want each person to succeed. Now you may better be able to understand why I make this analogy.

Withholding a person's passion will not only breed resentment, but also break one's spirit such that the passion will never again be publicly revealed. Doesn't it make more sense to naturally embed elements of the passion within the flow of the person's typical daily routines, and, possibly as an added incentive and in partnership with the person, build in a little something extra that would be gratifying to achieve? If you figure out how to do this successfully, I promise you will be loved for it, and, years from now, you will be remembered for your kindness as well.

The *Diagnostic and Statistical Manual*, which defines the diagnoses for autism spectrum experiences, calls for repetitive, restricted areas of interest as one criterion. Yet in so doing, it concurrently sets a negative precedent for "abnormality." Clinical interpretations of passions may include the belief that the interest is socially inappropriate or age inappropriate. If we subscribe to the philosophy of always presuming intellect, then we will offer the person with autism *age appropriate* materials, opportunities, and experiences. After all, you can only know what you've been exposed to. However, if the person holds dear the passion above all else, we must honor it as fully as we support the person themselves – regardless of whether it is seen as immature or age inappropriate.

I once attended a luncheon and sat at a table with two pediatricians who had a young son with autism. Naturally I asked about the boy's passion, to which they both responded by rolling their eyes and telling me his passion was for Barney, the purple dinosaur from the popular children's television program. My perception was that they had heard enough about Barney in their home, and that it was a topic of embarrassment. I asked how they were supporting their son's passion, to which they said they were trying to discourage him from it. I then asked them to suppose he were still passionate about Barney at age sixteen, and they both exclaimed in unison, "He'd better *not* be!"

("Yes, but what *if*," I thought. How much time and energy would be expended in trying to force the passion out of his life in the name of replicating normalcy?)

Passions may also be perceived as a hindrance in someone's life, with no real value or purpose, or as a clinical obsession or compulsion. Such perceptions lead to behavior plans to redirect and extinguish the passion. In being proactive and valuing one's passion, we need first to recognize it as a form of communication, and then to acknowledge it as good and acceptable to the person. Attempts to behaviorally extinguish the passion must cease immediately in favor of understanding its purpose and potential uses. Passions are ice breakers in initiating conversation. They are relationship builders and relationship menders as well.

Once after hearing me speak, a young mother related a story about her son's passion for *The Wizard of Oz*. She had been having great difficulty connecting with him. He spent much time watching a video cassette of the famous movie over and over again, and seemed interested in little else. Many of the aforementioned preconceptions were uppermost in her thoughts, until one day he surprised her by coming up quite closely to her face (which he had never done before), scrutinizing her, and demanding, "Are you a good witch or a bad witch?" In her wisdom (and having been exposed to the movie ad nauseam), this mom gave the *only* appropriate answer: "Who me? Why, I'm not a witch at all. I'm Dorothy Gale, from Kansas," which, of course, is the next line of dialogue from the film. She had passed the test. The little boy lit up and got so excited that he giggled peals of laughter, and responded with the next line. To their mutual delight, they went through the rest of the scene. The woman told me what a significant breakthrough this had been because her son had never before communicated so directly with her. He had invited her *in,* and she accepted the invitation on his terms such that they now shared a secret bond and a greater understanding of one another. *That* is the power of valuing someone's passions.

Relationships may also be cultivated through clubs and websites where others share like interests. If someone has an intense interest that they love more than anything, why not indulge it and foster development of social interactions (and potential friendship) at the same time? The internet, e-mail, instant messages, chat rooms, message boards and other such forums are outstanding and "safe" ways to explore relationships without the pressures, awkwardness, distractions and expectations of in-person social interactions. One can participate on one's own terms and in one's own time. Of course there are certain precautions about use of the internet, and these will need to be communicated in ways that are understandable to the person with autism. But so often we dismiss computer communications as anti-social because we have a single, set perception that "social" must occur face to face, and in person.

Such relationship building opportunities can also be relationship mending opportunities if a parent, educator or other caregiver facilitates such participation. It can be a learning time for all concerned, and a new beginning in the relationship. Valuing someone's passion in this way is self-validating. Because people identify so closely with their passions, it is tremendously gratifying when others take a genuine and sincere interest in eliciting further information about the passion. It validates one's purpose for being.

For the parents of the child who may never surrender his interest in Barney, I would perhaps advocate rethinking how he presents his passion to others as he grows older, such that he's not set up for failure and humiliation by his peers. This may mean gentle, respectful and private discussions about determining how much or how little to air the topic, as well as appropriate time and place. It may mean putting a positive "spin" on how the passion is presented to others, such that it is done with sophistication. Why not coach someone in discussing his or her passion from the perspective of a collector, historian, or archivist? More young people are becoming savvy about the value, rarity and collectibility of certain trading cards, beanie babies, dolls and toys. Discussing a rare, limited edition, foreign-market Barney collectible valued at over $300 may be better received by peers as opposed to the impression that the person is still "stuck on baby stuff." This may mean you having to assume the onus of investigating such an approach by surveying other collectors. Better still, offer to support the passionate person in connecting with like enthusiasts, particularly via the internet. If there are time constraints or parental expectations, perhaps the agreed "compromise" time for focusing on the passion becomes those opportunities to connect with other such Barney fans. This is positive social interaction, even when it occurs by e-mail.

Certain passions also have the potential to be grossly misinterpreted by others, causing undue concern and alarm. A father once approached me to discuss his son's interest in firearms, which was creating controversy at school. Before he could explain further, I interjected. I knew that this young man wasn't interested in guns from the standpoint of violence, destruction or doing harm. He was interested in them solely because of their mechanics of operation. He was fascinated with deconstructing them in order to better understand them. He also possessed a great respect for them. I urged the father to ensure that such distinction be made clear to those concerned at the school, while concurrently coaching his boy around certain cautions and the sophisticated spin (as noted above).

Another young man was fascinated with medieval devices of torture. This might create serious concern to anyone perceiving it at face value. But in discussing his passion, I readily understood that precisely deconstructing the mechanics of such devices was only a portion of his greater passion for religion and spirituality. His goal was to become a Christian missionary. Given that similar devices are still employed in some parts of the world, he sought to gain control in demystifying them in order to feel prepared should he ever find himself so persecuted for his teaching his message. This made perfect sense to me, although he was reticent about revealing this deeply personal explanation to others.

A twelve-year-old young man with Asperger's took pride in telling me directly that his passion was "gore," as in horror film special effects. Already wise, he comprehended the need to curtail such discussions by tempering the acknowledgment of those present with understanding that such topics could be offensive and off-putting. Here too, I could appreciate his perspective. At his age I became fascinated by the films *Psycho* and *Jaws*. But again I wasn't fascinated by their violence; I was fascinated by their construction. The staggering impact of the shower scene in *Psycho* lies in a brilliantly edited montage of small snippets of film, which, when assembled, give the impression of a brutal assault. Likewise, in *Jaws* I was most attentive to Steven Spielberg's unique timing and camera angles, to the extent that I wanted to become a film director. I scripted elaborate storyboards, recreated certain scenes in animation "flip" books, and walked through the house with my hand held to one eye, telescope-style, creating my own movies. (Understandably then, I was mildly miffed that the mother of the two small girls I babysat asked me to discontinue drawing them graphic depictions of sharks devouring luckless bathers.) I used my own analogy when trying to explain such an outlet to the worried mother of an adolescent girl who was intrigued by horror films. Perhaps in some way, an adolescent fascination with horror films is an outlet for venting vexations.

Some perceived passions might have deeper meaning in that they are more symbolic than simply an intense fondness. These will require an ability in caregivers to look beneath the surface to decipher the passion's true purpose. For example, one young woman was fascinated with people's shoes. The longer I talked with her team, the more it became apparent that she learned a lot about people, their personalities, and demeanor from the style and condition of their shoes, as well as from their walking stride and gait. She was gathering important information in a subtle, inconspicuous manner, as befitted her nature. She was also so painfully self-conscious that she spent a lot of time staring down at the floor, discreetly observing people's shoes.

I was also told of a young man who was passionate about apples. Again, through teasing out pertinent information from those who knew him best, we established the true origin of the passion. He was estranged from his mother, but during the time he lived at home with her, he had been accustomed to a diet that included lots of apples. Clearly, the apples were associated with his longing each time he held, smelled and tasted them. Given his communication limits, he independently discovered a way to conjure memories of a happier time with the one person in life he truly loved. The apples were a tangible, concrete way of reminiscing, just as others might turn the pages of a picture album or view a home movie. In each instance, the passion wasn't just about shoes or apples; it was about what they symbolized and represented.

As Temple Grandin reminds us, when someone's passions are valued and indulged, they are being encouraged to carve out their own creative niche that could possibly lead to vocation. I am not advocating that someone should engage in their passion for as many hours as they wish. Everyone has personal responsibilities to contribute and act upon within a structure and routine. However, one's existence will be greatly mollified if elements of one's passion transpire naturally throughout one's day. The onus of creating strategies by building on passions does not fall upon the individual caregiver. Each caregiver is a member of a team. There is much collective wisdom and expertise within each team that must be gently, and carefully coaxed. Remember: the person will guide us to what works for them.

As an exercise and within a group or team, brainstorm potential learning opportunities, avocations, and vocations for the following topics: wheels on vehicles (cars, trains, trucks and planes); astronomy; the PowerPuff Girls cartoon series; dinosaurs; people and places that have changed names over the years; cathedrals. Each represents a very real area of passion for one or more persons I have known. Consider how elements of each subject area could be imbued within the natural flow of one's typical daily routines.

Guiding Principles – Valuing Passions

- Respect and value personal passions

- If you understand how to build upon passions with learning opportunities you will be loved and remembered for it

- Passions are relationship builders, relationship menders, and are self-validating

- Support others' perceptions of a person's passion in proactive ways

- Passions may lead to potential avocations and vocations

- Be prepared to decipher the true intent of passions that are misinterpreted by others

Chapter 4

Preparing to Learn

Demystified for the reader in this chapter:

- Ways in which many people with autism think, learn and process information

- Strategies to support others feeling safe and comfortable and in control of knowing what's coming next

- Appreciating the art of self-accommodation

- Unraveling the riddle of repetitious "obsessive-compulsive" behavior

- Communicating the "social out"

- Some thoughts on the challenges of homework

In the planning of teaching and learning opportunities, we must ask some fundamental questions. First, is the situation conducive to learning, given what we know to be true about an individual's personal sensitivities to environmental stimuli? Without such an assessment, a person cannot be poised for successful interaction, engagement and response in an environment fraught with all of one's known "triggers". (Such sensory sensitivities, common to many folks with an autistic experience, are defined in Chapter 5.) Armed with such individualized knowledge, teams can develop an environmental checklist of sorts. It is then crucial to make physical adjustments, adaptations and accommodations to the learning environment wherever possible (be it school or the workplace). Many such adaptations are low cost or no cost, such as lessening the intensity of light in the area, or creating a learning carrel or partition for focus and privacy. Other considerations may involve reducing the number of distracting environmental visuals, adjusting the volume of the public announcement system, or giving people foreknowledge of fire alarms or break buzzers.

Second, is the learning opportunity functional such that it will make sense from the person's perspective? Instead of conceiving "special" programming, I advocate consideration of the typical curriculum or developmental achievements, and working backwards from that to tailor learning to the person's needs. As I've recommended, the very best way to address this is to start by building upon the person's passion(s). With elements of one's passions embedded within the flow of typical daily routines, the person may be motivated to learn as never before. It is also important to ensure that learning opportunities occur within the individual's natural environments, meaning those in which the person's typical peers live, learn, recreate and function within the community. Remember, we are all more alike than different and we all just want to be accepted and recognized by our peers and our communities.

In order to teach, it will be helpful to try thinking in ways similar to many of those with autism. We need to be mindful of the context within which concepts are taught and learned because of the potential for them to be forever linked to that specific situation. We must brainstorm strategies for generalizing such concepts to a variety of situations. The concept of being unable to disassociate this "linkage" is the same as when someone asks you: "Where were you when Kennedy was assassinated…when the Challenger space shuttle exploded…during the 2001 terrorist attacks on America?" Amazingly, you will be able to call up specific information about your precise activity at the time you received the news, no matter how long ago it was. But if the same person were to ask what you were doing the day, week or month before or after the exact time of the event, you would be unable to recall it. We do this with favorite songs all the time. When you unexpectedly hear a song you haven't heard for a long time, it immediately conjures up memories of people, places and events in your life at a time that you will forever associate with the song. We also associate smells with environmental memories in this manner.

Because of this strong associative cognition, sometimes the person with autism may have difficulty with perceptions of isolating numbers, words, letters, concepts or objects outside of the sequence in which they are learned. For a basic example, someone may readily recognize the letter D when it is partnered with its brothers, A, B, C, and E. However, when D is isolated separately, confusion may arise because there is uncertainty whether it is the same D as before. The person may wonder, "Does it have the same meaning and significance as it did before?" To understand, consider a similar concept. Think about the times when you have been given driving directions such as "Get off at the Pleasantville exit." When following the directions, you come upon an exit that says "Pleasantville/Fairvale." Now that there is an unexpected difference, do you take this exit, or will there be a separate exit which will state definitively Pleasantville? The person giving you directions may well have meant you to take the Pleasantville/Fairvale exit, thinking that you would know to do the same.

It might be helpful for the person struggling with the isolation concept to give them control in visually fading the "brothers" around the particular item (I'm envisioning a film lap dissolve of sorts). Give the person the ability to reverse the process as well. This could be as simple as removing or covering the "brothers" with pieces of paper, or as sophisticated as setting up a computer sequence controlled by the person.

As we've acknowledged, so many folks are visual thinkers. Remember the ancient proverb: I hear and I forget, I see and I know, I do and I understand. This makes perfect sense for people who will also learn visually. Our words dissipate into thin air soon after we've uttered them. They are intangible, not concrete. This is why people fail when given multi-part verbal instruction. You have reached step number four, and they're still trying to fully visualize what step number one should look like. If concrete visuals aren't provided to reinforce verbal direction, many folks need process time to make a "picture" in their mind of what you are discussing. What you think is obvious may not be perceived as apparent first and foremost. Reverse this thought, and think of it this way: I see the face in the cloud first, and the cloud second. You probably see the cloud first, and the face only if I take the time to point it out to you.

Making mind pictures also relates to the ways in which some people struggle to assimilate their understanding with typical peers. Remember when you discovered that the words you made up to bridge gaps in your understanding of the words to the Pledge of Allegiance, the National Anthem, or the Lord's Prayer weren't anywhere close to what people were actually singing and reciting? I used to think that an "elemeno" was a real thing. I thought an elemeno was a little brook or stream, which I saw in my head. It wasn't until much later that I realized the other children were saying "L, M, N, O." One friend told me of her son's special request while they were making orange construction paper pumpkin cutouts for Halloween. He asked, "Mom, when we're done with the pumpkins, can we make witchestands?" She had to confess that she was unfamiliar with those, to which he answered, "You know, like in school when we say '…and to the Republic, for *which it stands*'." You see, in his mind he already had one set perception of "witch" and associated it with all future connotations.

So often the people we know and care about are forever seen as recipients of services that we define. We need to ensure that reciprocation is embedded into learning opportunities. It can be both powerful, and empowering. How often do we think to give others the chance to demonstrate what they have to offer? My friend Pat Amos tells a wonderful and touching story about a chance reciprocal learning opportunity involving her son Dan:

> When my son Dan was very young, it was so hard to get a good interaction going between us. He was labeled

with all those scary diagnoses, but all I knew for sure was that he seemed very dis-synchronized. I felt like a dance instructor trying to get a novice with two left feet to dance. Then one day, when Dan was about six years old, we had a "Helen Keller" moment. You remember the story of how [Helen's] teacher helped put Helen's hand under the water pump, and Helen suddenly made a connection? In our situation, the connection wasn't prompted by water but a half-gallon of ice cream!

I was getting some ice cream – vanilla, Dan's favorite – out of the freezer, and Dan could hardly wait. Before I could put the ice cream in his bowl, he started digging into the box. I, always trying to follow his lead and get a response, asked, "Dan, did that taste good?"

He looked so excited that I had a moment of inspiration. I said, "Dan, I'm going to take my spoon and give you another taste. Then, you do it for me." He looked at me. He giggled. And he put a spoonful of ice cream in my mouth. You could just see all the cells in his brain light up.

We were in synch! I fed him. He fed me. We laughed so hard and ate that ice cream until we felt sick. I knew he had made an important connection, and finally understood how shared experiences can be fun. It may have looked strange or silly but he got it!

At that time, there was no way for me to know clearly what that experience meant to him or whether he realized he had made a breakthrough. I didn't get my answer until about five years later, when he suddenly said, "Remember when we fed each other that ice cream? Could we do it again?"

The first time we shared I thought it was a turning point. Later, when he reminded me of the experience, I realized it had meant as much to him as it had to me.

Many of us know full well that consistency and structure of routine is a key to successfully supporting someone with an autistic experience. However, caregivers and educators hold a lot of information about what's coming next that doesn't get shared with the person. This relates to the covert social code that has already been discussed – we think it's a "given" that some things are known or understood. We need to do better at preparing people for what's coming next so that they will be in the very best position to be ready learners. When consulting privately, I always recommend a personal schedule or calendar in order for someone to remain visually grounded and focused with respect to time and sequence of activities and events. It also gives the person some measure of control and independence without reliance upon and reassurance of others.

For people with mild forms of autism or Asperger's, I suggest a personal portable calendar that visually displays a month at a time, available from any office supply store, in which they may make their own written notations. Folks who are computer-savvy enjoy the synchronicity of Palm Pilot devices for timekeeping. For others, a simpler schedule with pictures is a better aid – a plain, discreet vinyl folder that will be inconspicuous in any environment (one with the words "_____'s Schedule" printed on the front cover is not helpful to that end).

Inside the folder, there should be no rings or pockets of any kind; if there are, remove them. What is wanted is a simple folder with a front and back cover. On the lefthand side of the interior of the folder, at the very top, write legibly (or use press-on type), "To Do." On the righthand side at the top write "Done." Running vertically down each side to the length of the folder affix two or three strips of Velcro. This is where the person's pictures for their daily schedule will be placed. Well in advance of implementation, a catalog of images will need to be developed, and maintained in a recipe or file box. A camera that produces small, instant photographs is best suited for this kind of schedule. (For some, the image size might be too small.) In any event, I am strongly encouraging the use of an instant camera because the person can be involved in taking their own pictures for the schedule, and there are immediate results that can support understanding of the cause and effect of the camera's use.

I am wary of a lot of icons because I think many of them are subjective in their interpretation, and may be difficult to discern. Icons are good for capturing some vague concepts that are not readily communicated in a photograph such as where someone might feel pain, but for the most part photos are going to best capture people and places in the person's life.

In advance of developing a catalog of images to be used, or in considering the activities one could enter in a personal calendar, I recommend breaking such activities into two separate categories: preferred and non-preferred activities. This means discussing with the person those activities they like best, and drawing upon that person's passions and interests (the preferred activities). The non-preferred activities are those that the person may not necessarily dislike but knows must be accomplished in order to proceed with the day. Acknowledge that the non-preferred activities are a means to an end: they connote assumption of personal responsibility; they're socially acceptable; or they fall within the realm of parental expectations.

Once the lists have been developed, it is now time to glean images and icons that will communicate these concepts. Each picture should also have the word or name written on it, and a small piece of Velcro affixed to its back for placement on the "To Do" side of the schedule. Only the pictures to be used for each day or set sequence of activities during a given day should appear on the schedule. The schedule is not the place to store one's entire catalogue of images.

It is mandatory when sequencing activities that they be sequenced in a preferred/non-preferred/preferred sequence. Otherwise there is no incentive for the person to become engaged, and the schedule becomes just another device in our arsenal of tools designed to regulate someone's life – and which they will resist. In fact, when introducing the schedule, it may even be best to start with two or three preferred activities before a non-preferred is introduced. (When the concept has been unsuccessful, I have discovered it was because it was implemented improperly.)

Every evening, before the person retires to bed, support them in arranging their schedule for *the next day*. That way, they can go to sleep feeling safe and comfortable, calm and less anxious about what tomorrow will "look like." For some, it may be too overwhelming to schedule the entire day (there may not be enough space to do so anyway), so simply schedule up until a natural break such as a mealtime or transition activity. It is best not to arrange the images or mark a personal calendar by specific timeframes. This will cause anxiety in creating a sense of rigidity and undue pressure to achieve the sequence within those times. (The exception may be in setting a parental time limitation on certain, occasional select activities.) The parent, educator or caregiver will guide the duration of each activity, unless the individual is capable of doing so on his or her own.

As each activity is completed, the person with the picture schedule is encouraged to lift the image from the "To Do" side, and place it, in sequence, on the "Done" side. Encourage the person writing in their personal calendar to check off or draw a line through a completed activity (much like those of us do with "To Do" lists – and feel a certain satisfaction in the completion). Personal calendars can also be used to mark coming events such as birthdays, anniversaries, social engagements, or doctor appointments. For others, "count down" to such dates by marking off a prominently displayed household wall calendar.

The most important part of using a personal schedule is to encourage the person in using it independently. Many educators already have such schedules posted in their classrooms, but too often children have to physically get up from their chairs to see what's scheduled next (stigmatizing them in front of typical peers), or the schedule is not personalized and used by the entire class. Even if the child has a schedule on the desk, it is usually not portable and the child is dependent upon an adult to sequence it, or the child must be in the room to view the schedule (which doesn't help the kid feeling "stuck" while in the hall en route to another room). The difference here is that the schedule is the personal property of the person, and it travels wherever they go: home, school, work, the community. After the initial introduction, it is to be controlled and maintained by them alone. If the person finds value in it (and I have yet to meet anyone who doesn't), it is a concept they will employ for the rest of their lives, much the same as many of us use personal schedules, calendars and Palm Pilots – and would be lost without such timekeeping devices.

One final thought about personal schedules. It is very important to build in breaks or "downtime" opportunities throughout the day. This will be a chance for the person to find private, discreet release from educational/vocational and environmental expectations. (Most typical folks do this naturally via bathroom, cigarette and coffee breaks or water cooler conversations; here it must initially be intentionally scheduled.) The classroom of one young student for whom I was consulting had a small tent set up at the back of a room divider, where it was fairly well camouflaged. (He was young enough that his periodic and brief absences from the rest of the class were not terribly distracting or noticeable.) At the agreed upon time, the boy could close himself up in the tent and independently manipulate a small hourglass timer for the duration of his downtime. (Even better would have been to make it understood that the tent was available for *all* students in the classroom.) This same team, though, experienced difficulty in understanding why the boy would need a break directly following what they perceived to be a break or "downtime" activity. I enabled them to realize that his one-on-one time with a particularly chirpy classmate, or playing out at recess, was *work* for him (i.e. maintaining composure and meeting behavioral expectations), from which he needed relief.

Beyond a personal schedule, there are many activities during the day – especially the school day – that are unstructured and undefined. Such activities include riding the school bus, recess, lunch, gym class, pep rallies, and other extracurricular activities. These are times when those with social challenges are most likely to struggle. Wherever possible, such an individual will be greatly relieved and welcoming of any sort of additional structured supports, such as a being a recess monitor, for example. Anything at all in which the person can be assigned a purpose will be very helpful. One should always have a sense of purpose, especially upon entering unstructured social settings. Some educators, already attuned to certain students' needs, have structured the lunchroom to include "lunch bunch" tables, the daily conversation of which focuses upon particular topics of discussion. The beauty of this concept is that no one person is singled out; the specific conversations are intended *for all students.* Similar opportunities could be offered through the development of clubs and other gatherings, perhaps inspired by those with similar passions.

Sometimes people give the impression of being something less than who they truly are because it is expected or assumed, or because it's safer. If everyone assumes you have learning differences, and interacts with you as a less than an equal partner, then there's no incentive (or trust) to reveal one's inner brilliance.[1] One gentleman wrote about his fear of exposing the "normalcy" that he could read. His staff read him the Easter Bunny story, while boundless thoughts about planets and life filled his head. He fought to cling to the one thing he could control: his façade of foolishness. Too often, and with all best intentions, we stymie others' growth by offering them only materials and activities suited to what has been declared as his or her "mental age" of functioning. I'm asking that we continually seek to broaden our collective horizons through new opportunities that are attractive and appealing, and correlate with one's chronological age.

I don't believe there is necessarily a value to grouping people with like disabilities together. Oftentimes, the person with autism is placed with persons with learning differences because they bear this diagnosis as well, or because of assumptions made about their intellect. While the person with autism will likely be compassionate and sensitive towards the others, that person will be ultimately unhappy at being displaced and intellectually unchallenged, and it will show. Sometimes it is helpful for small groups to band together if they are unable to tolerate the environment in which they must learn or work. However, the big world isn't so sensitive, and doesn't accommodate our needs. Consider discreet accommodations such as music earphones, earplugs, tinted windows or eyeglass lenses, or partitioned work areas to block or diminish environmental stimuli. Determine the optimal learning environment based upon what you know to be true of each individual person.

Some people have taught themselves to read, or to read material printed upside down (a gift known to astound staff on occasion). Some folks describe their experience as operating on separate tracks, which they have learned how to regulate to control their thinking, hearing, or vision. (Still others have been unable to sort that process through.) Some must carefully observe typical peer behavior in order to make an attempt at replicating it, like how any one of us can become a better artist through repeated copying and tracing. Sometimes – despite all our professional best intentions, wisdom and expertise – people figure out for themselves what they need to get by, and how to accommodate those needs in order to just fit in.

A friend of mine came to town for a speaking engagement, and asked to go out for ice cream the second night she was there. I was somewhat surprised by her request because, unbeknownst to her, I had been told that the night before she had gone out for ice-cream to the same establishment with disastrous results. She cannot tolerate high-pitched children's cries and screams. The local ice cream restaurant was crowded with tourists and families with small children – who were crying and screaming. My friend had been seated in a booth next to one such family, and, losing all patience, stood up and yelled, "Can't you control your kids! Can't you keep your kids quiet!" (Ironically, she was saying all the things that a lot of parents of kids with autism hear publicly from strangers.)

Given this, I was a bit uneasy about revisiting the scene of the incident. As we pulled into the parking lot, it quickly became apparent that the restaurant was no less crowded than I imagined it had been the night before. As we walked toward it, I wracked my brains trying to discern a way to get through the environment that awaited us. I needn't have troubled myself. Now that my friend *knew what to expect of the environment*, she understood how best to accommodate herself. She unzipped her belly pouch, pulled out her Walkman, placed the earphones on her head, and cranked up the music full blast! She had figured out how to adapt to the environment without any assistance. Now, looking into the ice-cream cooler, she was yelling to me over the music, "Oh look! They've got butter brickle ice cream and

Pocohantas birthday cakes!" She may have drawn as much attention to herself as she had the night before, but – most importantly – it worked for her.

The most independent use of self-accommodation is also the most readily recognizable. People with autism have had to find safety and trust in what they can control (which is often precious little). We know that many people engage in repetitive, predictable behaviors – the classic, clinical autistic stereotypes.[2] Indeed, it is common for people with autism to also have a diagnosis of obsessive-compulsive disorder. But the riddle of incessant rocking, the spinning coin, the twisting faucet, the flipping light switch, the flicking fingers and the opening and closing door lies in the very perseveration that causes us to seek to extinguish it: its predictability. *There is safety in sameness, and a comfort in what is familiar.* This is why you'll notice such behaviors intensify at times when someone is losing control, such as when they're happy, excited, anxious or distressed. (Why, then, is this deemed perfectly acceptable behavior for winning contestants on TV game shows or sports arena spectators?) To extinguish what is comforting without allowing for other safe and comfortable outlets only paves the way to destruction and rebellion. That is, if you seek to extinguish a repetitive, perseverative behavior without introducing a more acceptable alternative, it is a guarantee that something else will surface to take its place – and it might be a something else no one bargained upon. Offering options and opportunities that build on someone's most passionate interests leaves less time for perseveration.

I have already cautioned about using the terms "obsession" and "compulsion" to describe one's passions:

obsession meaning a thought process that cannot be controlled, and compulsion meaning an action that cannot be controlled. For the person who experiences these "disorders," the obsession or compulsion crosses a line, seeps over into the person's life and potentially creates harmful distraction. Unless someone's perseveration becomes a *clinically defined* obsession or compulsion that impedes upon an individual's daily routine and responsibilities, causing one to miss meals, lose sleep, withdraw from others, lose interest in passions, or creating harm to self or others, *we must allow for it.*

If the person does not experience a true obsession or compulsion, does this mean that we should be contented to provide them with the opportunity to spend the majority of his or her time engaged in activities such as flipping a light switch, twisting a faucet, or opening and closing a door? There must be room for compromise tempered with time constraints and expectations that are reasonable and typical of any one of us, given our needs, responsibilities and environment. But I certainly hope that someone's need to release stress and gain control in feeling safe and comfortable by privately flicking fingers within their own home would be condoned by caregivers. The compromise may come in a partnership about a *mutually agreed* time frame in which the person may need a little more or less, and can independently make that determination before moving on. I see this need most often in children coming home from school and adults coming home from work. These are people who have spent the day working hard to pass, fit in and get by as well as they can, and for whom such downtime is necessary. When it is not permitted, I learn of folks experiencing "meltdowns" because they are overwhelmed and have reached a breaking point.

Is it okay to stop and flick one's fingers in the middle of a typical classroom setting or publicly in the community? These are not the most ideal environments because it will attract attention to oneself in ways that perpetuate a stereotype. This is where compromise, adaptations and accommodations come into play.

One helpful way to temporarily allay the need to engage in perseverative activity is through a small touchstone or talisman of sorts; something personal and soothing selected by the person (*not* selected by someone else on their behalf – it won't have any meaning then) to be worn around the neck or discreetly kept in a pant's pocket or purse. The touchstone will most likely be a picture of someone or something very meaningful, or a favorite small three-dimensional object related to one's passion. In times of mild duress, the person should discreetly look at the touchstone, or simply touch it through one's clothing to know it's there and constant. The person should call up everything possible related to what the touchstone represents for them, and how that makes them feel. The concept is the same for those of us who wear a cross or wedding band, carry pictures of loved ones, or find safety, comfort and release in worry stones or rosary beads. For the person with autism who is being bombarded with temporary environmental stimuli, a touchstone may support one's ability to quell anxiety, stay focused and remain calm. A written social story will support the introduction of the concept. Helpful reminders will enable the person to practice employing the touchstone prior to full independence. One young man of Native-American descent selected a piece of Indian jewelry to wear around his neck. He perceived it as "protection," and was calmed and soothed by his sense of connectedness to the talisman, and all it meant to him.

Despite enhanced communication, personally mainained schedules that incorporate downtime, and touchstones, there will naturally be circumstances encountered by persons with autism that will unhinge them, and interfere with their ability to learn. These folks need to be able to express what I call "the social out." Many of us know that, as adults, there are very few social situations where we do not have the option of excusing ourselves (you can even get up and walk out of a dental exam if necessary). We know this because we have learned it via the covert social code. Others, who are not privy to the code, believe they have only one option: that they are compelled to remain in the situation no matter how upsetting, overwhelming or overstimulating. These are the folks who will quickly exhaust their coping strategies – which may include my recommendations – and revert to basic survival tactics like rocking while covering their ears, humming, or flicking their fingers. Their behavior will intensify and escalate to the point where it can no longer be contained, and they lose it and "blow." This is, of course, not helpful for anyone, and only further stigmatizes the person who wants to be inconspicuous in the first place! Please don't believe that the person with autism *wants* to find themself on the floor in the middle of Wal-Mart looking up at curious, laughing, whispering onlookers – no one wants that kind of attention. No one wants to become publicly undone this way.

To avoid such future incidents, and *prior* to participating in the potentially off-putting social situation, discuss with the person his or her "social out." This will be a mutually agreed-upon word, phrase and/or gesture that the person may use when they sense the potential to become overwhelmed (this also means holding a discussion about recognizing such symptomology within oneself). The communication may be, "Please excuse me," "I need a break," "I need to leave," or "I need to go home now." I am recommending that only one social out be selected and recognized by all caregivers. It may otherwise be too difficult and confusing for the person to try to "match" the appropriate social out with each specific situation, especially in a moment of duress.

The communication of the social out must be acknowledged and honored with immediacy – and not by stating "Can you wait a few more minutes?" or "We have to pay for this first" or "Hang in there a little bit longer." Those are all vague concepts that do not define *precisely* when the person may be relieved from the situation. Responding in such a manner also negates the entire purpose in communicating the social out. The person has already "held it together" for as long as they are able, and is fast approaching the breaking point. The person is not playing games or being manipulative. If the strategy is not of good service to the person, they will quickly discard it and revert to other ways of coping. Unless you wish to set them (and yourself) up for catastrophe, it is important to drop what you're doing and exit *now* (which may only be temporarily). It's better than contending with the alternative, and is the best, most respectful decision.

Once away from the setting, and if feasible in the moment (if not, then later on), try a one-on-one mini counseling session. Commend the person for maintaining composure under duress, thank them for employing the social out effectively, and review the symptomology of their experience. Did they maintain better/longer this time than on previous occasions? If so, how come? If not, why not?

Can a person abuse communication of the social out? Upon initial introduction of the social out concept, the frequency of its use may seem more than coincidental; but be cautious that the perception of manipulation may just be a test of trust to see if you will really keep your word and honor the communication. This should subside significantly once the consistency of trust has been established. If we're talking about a child, determining the motives for expression of the social out within the sidebar counseling session will aid a parent in separating true need from typical kid behavior. But when in doubt, err on the side of caution and respect the communication. Social stories will also aid the introduction of the social out concept. Remember to combine this concept with my previously shared recommendations for optimal success.

Teachers have asked me to expound upon an area of challenge concerning homework. Their observations center upon some children's inability to complete homework, whether it's outright (perceived) refusal, or expressed anxiety about the work itself. My best thinking is that there are several possibilities. First, the refusal to complete a homework assignment in full may stem from the child having become personally affronted by what is being asked of him or her. While many children with autism have communication and social challenges, they can be quite solid in their confidence of personal, precocious gifts and talents. If the child has demonstrated that they can master a concept, the sense of offense comes in being asked to demonstrate that capability in multiple, varied configurations, that is the homework. A compromise may be in granting permission for the child to do half the number of homework problems, but only if the homework is not going to be publicly reviewed aloud in class. If that's the case, we may need to be more creative in conveying why completing the assignment in its entirety is necessary, or in strategizing when to involve the child in the classroom recitations (such as staggering the order of the assigned homework problems). We don't want to further stigmatize the child by having peers perceive him or her as having special privileges, or by openly acknowledging that the child is different and unable to complete homework assignments.

This raises another point. Parents sometimes ask me if I think it's a good idea to make a presentation about their child's autism to his or her class. I am cautious about this because it highlights one person's differences mutually exclusive of others. Perhaps a better recommendation is to hold a discussion with the class about *all of our* collective similarities and differences. For this same reason, be judicious about the discreet use of aides in typical classroom settings. Unless the aide is assigned to attend to all students, there will be no other child who is shadowed by an adult except the child with autism, bringing him or her further stigma.

The second reason I believe young people struggle with homework is because of anxiety. As will be reiterated in

Chapter 6, many folks with autism internalize and visually replay their struggles with great intensity, which can be immobilizing for some. People will affirm to me that they *know* the child is capable of the work, thus creating stress, confusion and misperceptions on the part of parents and teachers. However, this is not about incapability. It should be understood that for anyone it can be overwhelming, stressful and seemingly insurmountable to be simulta-neously confronted with homework, impending tests, and assignment due dates – hence the sense of futility or anxiety over the inability to discern where to even begin. These students require the support of educators and parents in breaking down the tasks (organized *visually* on a timetable that becomes the child's property – perhaps the personal schedule), so that the assignments are scheduled in manageable portions. Reinforce that the child need only focus on the work scheduled for the allotted time slot.

Another reason why homework may present challenges is because of a "perfection mode" within which some folks operate. Remember, we're talking about people who are often "pleasers." The aforementioned tension and anxiety are magnified because of personally imposed pressures to comply with exacting accuracy. Such students (and people not of school age) need to be supported in understanding that *everyone* messes up and does things wrong. Parents, teachers, doctors and others in the person's life don't do everything exactly right all the time, and this is not a life or death situation (even though it seems as such to many children). Support an understanding about flexibility within rules as a byproduct of this discussion; the same rationale applies. Give someone the "permission" to lighten up and go easy on oneself by relating anecdotes about times you messed up as a child – and lived to tell about it.

With patient reassurance, practice and support, these strategies should help students and others feel poised for learning success at any age.

Guiding Principles – Preparing to Learn

- Be aware of the strong associative link in teaching–learning opportunities

- Many people with autism are visual thinkers–learners

- Allow for process time

- Ensure that reciprocation is an integral part of teaching–learning opportunities

- People need to know what's coming next

- The ability to self-regulate one's personal schedule is of lifelong value

- Breaks and downtime are essential

- Be mindful of personal sensitivities as they relate to the teaching–learning environment

- Appreciate, acknowledge and build upon self-accommodations

- There is safety in sameness and a comfort in what is familiar

- Unless the perseverative activity is a clinically defined obsession-compulsion, we must allow for it within fair compromise

- Honor one's communication of the "social out" with immediacy

- People with autism are our teachers

Endnotes

1   I am not suggesting or condoning that we interact with people with learning differences in ways that do not speak to intellectual partnerships. It's how we organize teaching/learning opportunities that might look different because of the nature of their difference. Our methods and approaches may vary.

2   Please don't refer to such activity as "stimming" or "self- stimulation." To me, this connotes some mindless, purposeless behavior. It is, in fact, just the opposite.

Chapter 5

Personal Wellness

Demystified for the reader in this chapter:

- Understanding and appreciating the impact of movement differences in people with autism

- The significance of pain

- Self-injurious behavior

- The importance of connecting with one's own body

- The impact of sensory sensitivities

- Spirituality

In seeking to support the whole person, we must be willing to explore natural, holistic means to support what someone experiences. All too often, we jump on the pharmaceutical bandwagon, seeking the medications that will correct, manage or control behavior without really understanding who the person is and what drives the "behavior." For example, just as we might place undue assumptions on someone who doesn't speak, make eye contact, or respond to our communication with immediacy, so too may we make similar judgments about people who can't control their bodies. We accept the tremors of Parkinson's disease, the spasms of cerebral palsy and the tics of Tourette's syndrome – which may very well be neurological cousins of autism. Interestingly, I have also met typical folks with dyslexia, another neuro-developmental difference, who share commonalities with people with autism. I believe Attention Deficit Disorder (ADD), Attention Deficit Hyperactivity Disorder (ADHD) and Obsessive-Compulsive Disorder (OCD) are cousins of autism as well.

But what of our friends with autism whose bodies operate on a separate track from their thoughts? (This is different from the aforementioned and intentional, protective perseveration.) I implore us to consider the experience of autism as we would cerebral palsy. Because one's own body presents differently and may operate beyond one's volition, it doesn't mean that one's intellect is necessarily impaired.

Just as we should not disregard a lapse in communicative response, we should not justify physical inattentiveness as non-compliant or challenging. Some people simply *must* move their bodies in order to attend. Barbara Moran says, "It's like scratching an itch. It doesn't mean you *enjoy* the scratching; you need to do it!" Still, others have difficulty "hitting the mark," and overshoot their target (the child who, when Mommy says "Give me a kiss," runs past Mommy and hits the wall instead). I have seen my friend Michael need to get up from his work table in order to run laps around the first floor of his home. Once he gets that "stuff" *out*, he is able to return to his work, focused and refreshed.

For others, it is to experience the "song in your head" syndrome. Many of us have had the experience of repeatedly hearing a song throughout the day and perhaps even being awakened by it during the night. Try as we might, we are unable to exert the control necessary to banish it. For some people with a movement difference, the "song in your head" is in their entire body, and they have no more control to regulate it than you did when "stuck" with the repetition of the song. This also relates to one's inability to produce verbal speech at will.

Often, people are relieved if you simply abandon your demands and expectations, and meet them where they are in the moment, literally in the movement. This means engaging in the same rocking motion yourself alongside the person. This can be a strong visual cue for some, and a lovely non-verbal social interaction for others. Gentle words will be helpful at this time. Your acknowledgment of the rocking is validating, and promotes confidence in the person's ability to move forward by transferring his or her initiative to your will, with your body as the visual guide. Touching someone on the elbow, or gradually moving slightly in front while maintaining the motion, will break the spell. This concept of yourself as the visual guide or beacon enables some folks to independently walk about unfamiliar places; for them, you are cutting a path ahead through the fog.

Physically shifting from one floor surface to another, through a transom, or from lightness into darkness – no matter how subtle – is to face environmental change that may betray one's ability to move forward. Anne Donnellan and Martha Leary have accomplished an inordinate amount of research on movement in people with neurological differences, and I strongly encourage the reader to pursue their work. (Please refer to one such reference work, as listed in the Bibliography under "Hill, D.A. and Leary, M.R."). Physical therapists and occupational therapists can offer suggestions for exercises and activities designed to promote acquisition of enhanced fine and gross motor control; but isolated therapy sessions will do little unless the concepts are embedded within the flow of the person's typical daily routines. In this way, the person with autism can employ the recommended techniques in a natural way, free from interruption of their day, while building upon what they would ordinarily be doing.

Sometimes the movement someone engages in may cause them harm and self-injury. While I've previously made a plea for leniency in permitting folks to engage in their individual coping activities, we cannot allow them to harm themselves (nor do they wish to either). The *very first* course of action in providing such intervention is to rule in or rule out the potential for the person to be experiencing physical pain and discomfort, which bears down upon and exacerbates what they are already experiencing as a person with autism. *Pain affects behavior.* You know this if you recollect your mood during a migraine, menstrual period, ulcer, ear infection or toothache. When any one of us has experienced pain associated with such ailments, we usually feel more sensitive to noise and temperature, become moody and irritable, or "shut down" and withdraw from others.

For someone without a consistent, understandable and reliable method of communication, their expression of pain and discomfort (or the attempt to nullify it) may result in physical aggression, belligerence, and self-injury, such as hitting the side of one's own face because of a dental impaction. I have known of persons wrongly diagnosed and subdued with antipsychotic medication for aggressive or self-injurious behavior who were later discovered to be in tremendous physical pain because of an undiagnosed medical ailment. Once properly treated, the identified behavior ceased, though it was previously thought to occur for "no apparent reason." Be aware, too, that such chronic, ongoing pain can't help but eventually deteriorate someone's mental health.

I have often heard it said that people with autism "don't feel pain," or at least don't interpret it as most others do. I'm not wholly convinced of the validity of such statements. I have discovered that people do, of course, experience pain; they just may not have the words to put to it, or don't know they are *supposed* to report it. I have known of people who exist with intense pain – even broken limbs – and don't realize that they can be treated and cared for. My message to these folks has been to reinforce that it is not OK to endure unreported pain and discomfort.

Foods and the combination of certain foods can trigger internal explosions of delight and angst. Acid foods such as citrus fruit, strawberries and tomato-based products can induce these sensations. Food preservatives, chemicals and dyes can create painful allergic reactions as well. Many people with autism have severe reactions to casein (dairy) and gluten (wheat-based) food products. When in doubt, and with the person's *informed* consent, remove the suspect food for a specified period of time to note any trends in wellness. Consult with a well-informed dietician or nutritionist for a diet review. There are many nutritional supplements, substitutes and alternatives available. Additionally, it is very common for folks with autism to experience gastrointestinal issues that create gas, bloating, constipation, severe cramping and bowel impaction. Often, the cause is an intestinal tract bacteria that can be eradicated with proper treatment. Be cautious, though, of the equally painful side effects of certain antibiotics.

Allergies of all types and even sinus infections are very common in people with an autistic experience. This incurs physical pain and discomfort through headaches and migraines, sinus pressure, red, itchy eyes, runny nose, and ear blockages. You may be surprised to learn how many people don't realize that it is not normal to feel this way routinely and that relief is available for the asking.

If pain has been unequivocally ruled out, then we must observe and document the times when the person is *least likely* to engage in the harmful behavior, and incrementally build more of those opportunities into his or her schedule. In extreme situations, and despite the person's ability to communicate, some folks have descended into a vicious cycle of physical restraints (being forcibly, physically controlled) and mechanical restraints (intended to achieve the same effect through straps, wraps, cloth mitts, or other devices designed to restrict movement). This is, of course, an absolute last resort and an interim only in lieu of continuing, positive interventions. It is certainly not desired for its antiquated, dehumanizing approach. Trying to get at *why* someone would want to harm him or herself by asking them that question isn't helpful either; if they knew, they would stop. If you press, you'll get a pat answer – the one you might be expecting, but an answer that is not truthful.

One lovely young teenage woman could not resist from hitting her face at every opportunity, to the extent that she was in danger of causing permanent physical damage to herself; and yet she was the first to communicate, "I hate my hands." It was heartbreaking to witness her struggling with something bigger than she was. She experienced the restraints discussed above and more, at one point being wrapped in sheets virtually around the clock. The horror of this occurring in this day and age is that, again, the focus becomes the behavior and the person is lost. I wept when I learned of her deep attachment to a certain pillow that she had named. It was the only constant in her life during those long hours, and she spoke with the pillow, like a person, for comfort. She also wore a splint-like device on both arms so that she could not bend her elbows to reach her face.

Recently, a provider in a community residence who has a strong commitment to serve her, and is well grounded in person-centered philosophy, received the young woman. She still struggles, but the splints are gradually being faded. What has intrigued me is that at bedtime she dictates to her staff a precise sequence for tucking her into bed so that she can get through the night without harming herself. This involves grasping a pillow in each arm, and having the bedding tucked in tightly on either side. Even at times when she's felt uneasy about going to sleep, she has communicated her need for staff to remain with her until she drifts off. My question has been: How is it that she knows precisely what she needs in order to get through the night successfully, but is seemingly unable to do so during waking hours? Does it have something to do with going it alone? Is it an issue of responsibility for control? Such questions are often unresolved, even by neurologists. The young woman is a kind and gentle human being with a supportive, involved family and so much to offer. I am optimistic for her future.

Lack of coordination and physical awkwardness are also clinical hallmarks of autism spectrum experiences. People need the opportunity to engage with their bodies, to connect with their own limbs, and to become empowered to tame what can be willfully tamed. Any exercise program offered should begin with *self-contained, non-competitive activities.* This doesn't mean that these activities necessarily need to occur without a partner; it's just that there should be no winner or loser – and no undue pressure to succeed or perform within a set timeframe. The physical activities at which many folks with autism best excel include walking; running; gymnastics; ballet and dance; yoga; swimming (hugely important – water is very meaningful to many, perhaps for the overall pressure it offers); horseback riding; bike riding; weight training and martial arts, which has an appealing regimen and promotes self-discipline. Adding favored music to any of these activities will be a pleasing enhancement.

Connecting with one's own body also promotes one's ability to eliminate bodily waste regularly. Some simply don't "feel" the sensations associated with the urge to evacuate waste, and need gentle support through diet and exercise to do so. Others have such precious little control in their lives that refusing to release one's waste becomes a coping mechanism. Social stories explaining the process of waste elimination are crucial to further understanding of the body's function and knowledge of what becomes of the waste is important as well. People need know that they are not shedding a living, vital part of the body (which can trigger panic and fear). The person also needs support in understanding that it is desirable and healthy to eliminate waste, and that everyone they know does this (family, teachers, staff, doctors, etc.). It is not a weakness or sign of imperfection to eliminate waste, and such personal well being will waylay future health problems. When I was a young boy, using the bathroom at school was never a consideration for some of these same rationales, including fear of getting lost. At the end of one day in first grade, I was so focused on getting home to urinate that I didn't hear the teacher tell those children who walked home to sit down because we hadn't stood in unison. I was the only one left standing, and upon admonishment from the teacher I promptly sat and wet my pants (but never told anyone). Other times, I would deny having to use the bathroom when adults inquired about my squirming agitation as if it were an admission of fault to confess it was true.

We must also support, understand and appreciate sensory differences in people who experience autism. Consider the sensory overload some people experience while trying to assimilate everything around them in order to just "fit in." We know that noise can be overwhelming: people coughing, clapping, laughing or sneezing; dogs barking; children's shrill cries; airplanes overhead; car doors slamming; the roar of a vacuum cleaner. Unanticipated noise is assaultive and frightening – it is uncontrollable and unpredictable. However, loud, repetitive noise, music or videos *controlled by the individual* may be sought out, perhaps for reasons of safety and comfort, as we've discussed. The wearing of personal Walkman music players is mainstream for so many people; the use of such headphones may be very helpful for folks so sensitive to the potential noise of certain environments. For others, small, discreet foam earplugs may be an option.

Some people pursue the path of Sensory Integration therapy. I cringe when I think of caregivers scheduling time to run a hairbrush over someone's skin – no one else does this during his or her day. Use the concepts of Sensory Integration and embed them in the natural flow of someone's typical daily routines using everyday devices. Look for opportunities to engage and gently desensitize someone through massage at bath time, or helping to fold towels, warm and fresh from the dryer, for example.

Touch can be overwhelming and intrusive, or desirable in the form of a tightly swaddled blanket or the "deep pressure" burrow of sofa cushions and mattresses. Many of us know someone who will beg us to sit or stand on them, or ask to be rolled up in a throw rug. When in doubt about touch, ask permission of the person. We so want to be liked and accepted that we sometimes get overzealous, and become too "touchy-feely" too soon, which is off-putting. I recall one pediatrician who promoted his brand of intervention for initiating interaction with young, seemingly disinterested kids with autism. He said it's best to get in real close to a child, pick them up, roughhouse, and rustle their hair to elicit (read "force") an interaction. I remember thinking to myself, "If you *ever* did that to me, I would bite you so hard you would know never to do it again!"

The respectful choice is, of course, to be patient and await an indication that you have been invited "in." One such instance occurred for me while visiting with a young man focused on twirling a long piece of nylon rope. I approached him slowly, speaking in smooth, low tones, and sat near to him, which he allowed. In due time, *he* moved closer to *me*, and began twirling his string in *my space*. This was my invitation in – it was that subtle – and a mutually shared, non-verbal communication began. The invitation in may even be as subtle as the person with autism *initiating* direct eye contact. Such fleeting nuances are often overlooked.

Too much light, particularly fluorescent lighting, is an extreme irritant for some people, and can distort perception. It is a harsh, abrasive, unnatural light that can be physically draining to endure for long periods; for some it is like the blare of a trumpet pressed up against the ear. There is no rule that says every bank of fluorescent lights in a school classroom or work area must be turned on. Turn off the bank of lights over the area where the individual sits, or rely upon lamps and natural light – everyone will like it better! As many of you already know, overhead fluorescent lights often have a buzz to them which is not always readily perceptible except to the very sensitive. One accommodation (if turning down the lights is not an option) is to offer the person amber or other-tinted lenses to wear when it becomes unbearable. Sunglasses in bright sunlight will also be a must for some.

Certain smells – food smells in particular – cannot be habituated so that they dissipate like the smell of an onion does after we slice into it. They remain constant and must continually be dealt with as fresh and anew, causing some folks to become physically ill. When one becomes so overwhelmed – and with no means to communicate it – the manifestation of the "behavior" transpires for what may be interpreted as "no apparent reason." Similarly, the texture of certain foods may be extremely distasteful. Such foods usually have "slimy" textures, like Jello, pudding, tapioca, or peanut butter; or are of a hard, crunchy consistency, like carrot and celery sticks. Some people, particularly children, restrict themselves to a few "safe-to-eat" foods, which may cause alarm for parents and caregivers. I am not, though, concerned with a rigid, self-imposed diet limited to a few select foods if the person isn't losing weight and is taking a vitamin supplement. To force food will create an otherwise avoidable battle. Often, the person will "venture out" on his or her own to sample, test and try new tastes and textures when they are ready.

Some folks may experience tactile sensitivities to clothing, wearing sweatshirts inside out because otherwise the sensation of cloth against skin is like sandpaper. Many people with autism will also tear labels off clothes for similar reasons, if a caregiver doesn't know to excise them to begin with. Some folks need clothes – particularly underwear – washed multiple times to soften the fabric before donning them can be a consideration. Others simply cannot tolerate certain fabrics. Why, then, does the offending article of clothing end up back in someone's closet or dresser drawer? It needs to be disposed of because the person is no more likely to wear it the next time it's offered. Otherwise, such situations have potential to escalate into power struggles.

I recall once being approached by two women who wanted to know where they could find a heavy-duty rocking chair for a gentleman they supported in an adult workshop setting. He had already worn out several chairs with his intense rocking and they were afraid he was going to rock too hard and injure himself by falling backwards. In questioning them further, I soon understood that this was not about finding the right chair; this was about assessing this man's environment and appreciating how overwhelmed he was by external stimuli, so he found safety and solace in rocking. This example is quite typical of how many folks approach situations, so bent on pressing a square peg to conform to a round hole without recognizing the obvious. This isn't about "fixing" the person to comply with the impossible; it's about assuming responsibility in assessing what is going on *around* the person so that respectful adaptations and accommodations can be explored in earnest.

What we need to understand is that the sum total of such sensory sensitivities can be an intensely debilitating and assaultive experience, causing people excruciating pain. Whenever anyone cannot reliably and understandably communicate his or her experience in the moment, there is always the potential for things to escalate and lose control. We may then make many assumptions and use phrases unjustly, such as "for no apparent reason," or "non-compliant behavior." It is important, then, to strive for exacting consistency in how we support someone to shave, brush their teeth, and wash and comb their hair. These are often very challenging activities for the person being supported. Their sensitivity will always be present to some degree, but what we must recognize is that each caregiver supporting the individual approaches each activity differently *every time*, so that an anxious situation is enhanced by the unpredictability of the sequence of steps.

Consider offering those wellness activities marketed to us all, and intended to de-escalate moods and anxiety through relaxation and release, such as: massage (if not by another human being, then by a piece of equipment controlled by the person); relaxation tapes of music or pleasing environmental sounds; long, warm baths; and aroma therapy incense or body gels.

Let us also consider each person's inner spirituality. I have yet to meet someone with autism who is not an inherently spiritual being – not necessarily religious, but spiritual in recognizing and deeply appreciating the beauty in everyone and everything about them. Many folks have a heightened awareness and exquisite sensitivity so that they are also clairvoyant. It is not at all uncommon for people with autism to perceive spiritual entities and angels about them and others; to know what a loved one is thinking; to receive premonitory information; or to see the colors of one's aura. Others may feel "displaced" in time, making connections to grandparents and older adults (and even their photographs) especially significant. Extreme caution and discretion is needed in selecting to whom such information is revealed, as there is great potential for such experiences to be labeled as "psychotic" or "hallucinations."

I have become close to Michael Hricko, my young friend who experiences so much of what I have shared. He is my hero. I lovingly think of Mike as I would Pinocchio, because Michael's ambition is to become a "real boy" (his phrase). His is an admirable and noble goal, and one that others with autism have opted not to achieve because it is safer not to, or simply insurmountable. But how does one become a real boy? There is no handbook that tells us step by step in logical progression how to become a real boy. Mike must copy and trace and observe very closely exactly what it is that other little boys do, say, react to, and take pleasure in. He is not alone in his quest. He has the sensitive, respectful support of his family and friends. For Mike, an "autism program" was unbearable. He is still struggling to cope with its repercussions. We know that one size does not fit all, yet we continue to advocate for universal models that have been successful for some, even though they may not be for others.

Michael and I have developed a bond that is not readily explainable. He has flattered me by saying, "All I am is in who you have become" and "I trust your heart like mine." We openly ponder the virtues of altruism, its beauty, and the power of its sentiment. We reflect that altruism is so rarely obtainable, particularly when we expect it from those who say they are there to support our goals. This is part of Mike's great struggle, but his sense of spirituality provides him impetus.

Michael's mother gives him the gift of open and honest expression, even at the risk of hurting her own feelings. Although Mike feels like a trapped tiger, forever pacing, he is patience personified in waiting for his team to coalesce. Presently, his team is fragmented into shards of glass, awaiting careful placement into Michael's mosaic. And in his inner placidity, Michael is forgiving and accepting, and still he waits. He waits for others to make up their minds to listen to him, and act on his words. In the interim, Mike advises that it is for us to continue the fight for what is right and true. In my eyes, Mike has always been the real boy he seeks to become.

I tell Michael that I have great expectations for his future as a visionary and advocate. His passion lies in God, and I envision him at a pulpit or lectern, shifting people's thinking and moving them toward what is right and true and good and kind. I am hopeful that some day Michael will also

initiate a movement that supports individuals with autism —
not from a programmatic perspective — but from a
standpoint that shows we've *really* listened. If anyone can do
it, Mike can.

Guiding Principles – Personal Wellness

- Appreciate that people's bodies do things they can't necessarily control

- Be willing to meet someone where they are in the moment to support them becoming "unstuck"

- Pain affects behavior — rule it out first and foremost

- People with autism are innately gentle beings who do not wish to harm themselves or others

- People with autism are exquisitely sensitive beings, and are routinely assaulted by their sensory sensitivities

- Respect and appreciate one's need for inner spirituality

Chapter 6

Mental Health

Demystified for the reader in this chapter:

- The significance of mental health issues among people with autism, and the stereotypes it perpetuates
- Understanding how to observe, document and communicate information about mental health issues
- Why mental health issues stymie all our efforts
- Acknowledging and supporting anxiety and Post Traumatic Stress Disorder

Allow me to make a disclaimer at the outset of this chapter. I am not a doctor, and I do not have the clinical authority to make mental health diagnoses. What I am relating here – at times quite emphatically – is based upon my personal experience and that of my colleagues. My goal is to explore an area of supporting those with autism that is all too frequently left unturned. My hope, as always, is to encourage others to consider a range of possibilities in an effort to shift our collective thinking.

In my experience, when someone with autism is challenging to support, there are three reasons. First, they have no consistent, reliable, and understandable means of communication accessible to them at all times. Second, they are in great (likely undiagnosed) physical pain and discomfort. Third, they are struggling with mental illness. The latter two contentions are, of course, subsets of communication if someone is unable to express their experience in the moment. We've already discussed the great importance of communication and pain issues, leaving mental health yet to be explored. However, before exploring mental health issues, it is mandatory that any medical condition causing chronic pain has been ruled out. A thyroid imbalance can also mimic symptoms of mental illness in its manifestation.

There has been a movement in the developmental disabilities field over the past decade to dispel and vanquish certain stereotypes about people with autism and learning differences, and mental illness. The late Dr Robert Sovner, a psychiatrist who specialized in supporting people with different ways of being, has been acknowledged as a leader in this paradigm shift. Such right-thinking clinicians maintain that mental illness is an equal opportunity offender, incapable of distinguishing a typical brain from one with different wiring. Therefore, *everyone* is fair game, regardless of one's perceived level of functioning. The distinction lies in how the manifestation of symptoms *appear* in someone with a difference, which often look dissimilar from the accepted clinical criteria of the same illness in someone who is "typical."

This belief flies in the face of traditional psychiatric support of people with autism and other differences. The longstanding, frequently unwavering, and still current belief is that the manifestation of challenging behavior (the "stuff" I previously said gets everyone's immediate attention) is a function of the autism, purely by virtue of being autistic. Many in the psychiatric community maintain that aggressive or dangerous "behaviors" are merely a byproduct of autism. However, you don't medicate autism; you don't medicate what someone experiences naturally any more than you would medicate cerebral palsy, learning differences, or blindness. What might be medicated is the adjunct residue of the experience – mood disorders, anxiety, trauma – as we will discuss, but only after all positive approaches have been exhausted. As such, people with autism continue to be misunderstood by the psychiatric community. Many remain undiagnosed with mental illness; others bear inaccurate or inappropriate diagnoses such as schizophrenia, schizoaffective disorder, intermittent explosive disorder, personality disorder, oppositional defiant disorder, and others. (I've also known folks with just a learning differences diagnosis who, in hindsight, were clearly autistic.)

What we must recognize, though, is that such diagnoses are rare in the general population but commonplace labels for persons with different ways of being. If we subscribe to Dr Sovner's contention, then this makes no sense. What does make sense is that the most prevalent mental illness among the general population is also the most prevalent mental illness for other folks. This bears true in my own work, in that of my colleagues, and in the work of other professionals who support folks with autism and mental health issues across the country. What we understand is that there is a great propensity for folks with different ways of being to experience a co-occurring mood disorder, specifically bipolar disorder (being comprised of both mania and depression) in addition to forms of anxiety and often post traumatic stress disorder.

Curiously, the *Diagnostic and Statistical Manual* (the clinician's bible for ascertaining psychiatric diagnoses) requires a diagnostician to rule in or rule out the potential for mood disorder diagnosis first and foremost. Why, then, are folks with differences seemingly the exception to the rule? This is because of stereotypes, and because of the belief that, in order to make an accurate diagnosis, one must reliably self-report one's own symptoms. Many people with autism are not in the best position to self-report for many reasons already discussed. They are, then, dependent upon others reporting information on their behalf – parents and caregivers. When this occurs, all the "stuff" that has people up in arms comes pouring out through well-intentioned venting about verbal and physical aggression, property destruction and self-injury.

What happens next is that the psychiatrist, observing the person's behavior, and being vulnerable to the information provided by caregivers, must make a number of professional judgment calls (because none of psychiatry is an exacting science). When people report *behaviors*, such as those mentioned, a psychiatrist has over seven hundred potential diagnoses from which to consider because of behavioral commonalities. But when we start by knowing to rule in or rule out the potential for mood disorder, we are far better equipped to share information that is defined by *symptoms* and not behaviors. The intent is not to make psychiatric presumptions; we should never presume to tell any doctor their business. The intent is to become good observers, more knowledgeable and better prepared for an open discussion with the psychiatrist.

As part of all my initial consultations, I always explore the potential for someone to be experiencing a mood disorder (granted, after all the person-centered discussion). I am disinterested in hearing about all the "stuff" someone has been manifesting; that's already a given (hence my presence), and it's disrespectful to rehash it in front of the person. What I am interested in learning about are syndrome-specific symptoms that could be indicators of mood disorder. In order to do so, I begin by asking for any anecdotal information about the symptoms we know are only ever specific to depression, and the symptoms that are only ever specific to mania – the two components of bipolar disorder, although there are a number of supporting symptoms that will remain to be explored with the psychiatrist.

It is very important to acknowledge to the person and his or her caregivers that the symptoms of a mood disorder are most often beyond the control of the person experiencing them, and *are not the fault of the person*. This is the most difficult preconception to overcome in order to be objective, particularly if you've been the target of aggression. We must recognize that this experience is not desired by the person, and is not a fun time (for anyone)! I use the analogy of being in a car to better explain it. When we drive a car, we sit in the driver's seat, at the wheel, and in control of the vehicle. The person with the mood disorder is constantly competing with the illness for the driver's seat.

Sometimes the person with the mood disorder is in the driver's seat, in control. Sometimes they're in the passenger seat, and can have some influence over the driver (a.k.a. the mood disorder). Other times they are in the back seat – as the driver races at top speed – out of control and completely at the mercy of the illness.

Because of their differences and the ensuing anxieties and frustrations endured, folks with autism are tremendously vulnerable to mood disorder. It is extremely important to note that the symptoms *must be* significant differences in the person's behavior; that is, a change from what is typical, and how you've known them to be. Think on this: Is there a presence of cycles? Do the cycles seem to fall at the same times annually? I have known many families and caregivers who have referred to "good" and "bad" times of the year, or that someone hits a "cycle" after a certain holiday or anniversary. Genetics can influence someone's vulnerability also. Is there a family history of mental illness, bipolar disorder, or alcoholism/substance abuse (a way of self-medication which may mask mental illness)? Both mania and depression can manifest in milder forms (hypomania and dysthymia); depression can also stand alone, existing without the presence of mania. Mania doesn't stand alone without periods of depression.

Consider organizing symptoms in the following manner. Symptoms must coexist together in "clusters."

Possible symptoms of depression

- *Crying, weeping, wailing, whining, moaning or general sense of sadness and melancholy, longer than two weeks in duration, and not post-loss (meaning not following a death or significant life-changing event, after which it would be typical to mourn).* Do not underestimate someone's exquisite sensitivity over a loss. The person with autism cannot "snap out of it," "shape up," or "get over it" in reaction to a situation that others may consider trivial or insignificant. Such persons may grieve losses that are not readily perceptible. They may dwell upon morbid thoughts about funerals, disease, death and dying; or not wanting to be seen as "different" and wanting to be accepted with "regular people." The person may make self-deprecating remarks such as "I hate myself," or "What's the use," or "No one loves me," or "I'm not wanted here." For someone who doesn't speak, this may manifest in self-injurious behavior such as scratching their flesh or banging their head.

- *Decreased interest in pleasurable activities.* This symptom should be quite distinct in its presentation because the person has lost interest in their passion. They pass up opportunities to participate in related activities, or intentionally miss such participation in favor of isolation or seclusion from others. (This includes doing something in order to be forcibly excluded.) This person may also give away or destroy materials related to their passions or other items meaningful to them.

- *Supporting symptoms.* These may include increased agitation and irritability; psychomotor retardation (a general, noticeable "slowing down," fatigue, and difficulty in movement such that one must exert great effort in order to accomplish the smallest of physical feats); "clinginess," where the person wants to physically "hang" on you, and needs repeated protective assurances; the person may have difficulty sleeping, and may sleep excessively (their sleep habits may also reverse so that they sleep during the day to avoid interacting with others, and spend their waking hours during the night); changes in diet, such as loss of appetite, feeling nauseated at the sight of food or placating oneself with excessive food; and the person may be so confused, listless or disoriented that they urinate in peculiar spots.

Possible symptoms of mania

- *Euphoric or irritable mood (with increased intensity of laughing, smiling/grinning and teasing behavior).* The person may seem delirious or giddy or his or her tolerance threshold for sensory sensitivities may be vastly diminished, heightening irritability. At times the person may have a fixed grin while speaking that appears unnatural and forced, and his or her speech may be pressured (hard and fast) as though his thoughts are racing. The person may force laughter at inappropriate times such as during solemn and serious topic discussions. If this person has always been a comedian of sorts, you will notice them taking things too far, being unable to cease the joke telling or physical slapstick so that it gets out of hand or causes harm.

- *Inflated self-esteem or grandiosity.* In the typical populations, these are symptoms that have become classic fodder for sensational tabloid journalism; that is, those folks who believe themselves to be Jesus

Christ, Hitler, or some other "larger than life" public figure. They may believe that they are receiving secret communications from radio and TV announcers intended exclusively for them; that they are at the epicenter of an international espionage plot; that they are related to a celebrity (or, if female, carrying a celebrity's love child, despite no symptoms of pregnancy); or that they are possessed of superhuman strength and powers (we've all heard stories of people who, believing they could fly, have jumped to their deaths from the roofs of tall buildings).

In someone with autism, grandiosity may manifest in a sense of omnipotence or belief that they are a fabled personality such as Santa Claus, the Easter Bunny, or a TV, movie or comic book character, or they may assume all or part of an authority figure's name; of desiring to hire and fire adults (parents, staff, police, doctors) or being able to control their salary; in resisting and openly defying authority (one young woman accused her father of molesting her, which, after proper investigation, was unfounded and revealed to be one symptom of manic grandiosity); in damaging property; in attempting to lift, pick up and throw heavy objects or pieces of furniture that they would *ordinarily* know are well beyond their means; in climbing up on the top of furniture, window sills, counter tops and cabinets, or out onto rooftops; in throwing and smearing feces, or in urinating in places other than the bathroom (*and* these folks would ordinarily know not to engage in this behavior); of hoarding or taking others' food at meals, even though the person has the same portions in front of them; and in harming loved ones – persons very dear to them, and whom they would not otherwise consider hurting. It is very important to note that afterwards, the person with autism is almost always remorseful for his or her actions during the times they were not in control. This is a *very common* reaction in people who are innately gentle beings.

Grandiosity may also manifest in that one receives purely auditory information, like the young man who believed Elvis was talking to him. When viewed in isolation, this might be interpreted as a hallucination, or psychotic episode, but when correctly perceived as an element of grandiosity, it fits perfectly as a symptom within a cluster of symptoms indicative of his bipolar experience.

- *Increased intensity of interest in pleasurable activities.* These will be the times when the person's passions may appear to be obsessions or compulsions. The person will become very intent in his or her focus and cannot be dissuaded from the activity, such that they will behaviorally escalate and lash out when compelled to do so. This may also be a time when the person's perseverative coping mechanisms intensify – violently rocking back and forth, for instance. For some, this symptom will manifest as an increased intensity in sexual behavior, such as masturbating inappropriately or with greater frequency, or engaging in dangerous, promiscuous sexual behavior (which the person would *ordinarily* know to avoid or would exercise informed caution).

This "hypersexuality" may manifest in someone making very provocative statements, or – if without speech – the person may pull on his or her underwear very hard, or put their hand down their pants frequently.

- *Supporting symptoms.* These may include increased agitation/irritation (including a "short fuse"); increased psychomotor activity (the person may seem "wired" and can go without sleep or minimal sleep for long periods of time, sometimes days in a row); changes in eating habits (the person's appetite has increased such that they gorge or hoard large quantities of food); flight of thoughts or ideas (jumping from topic to topic without any apparent connection between them, or being physically indecisive, moving from one activity to another without any correlation between them); and racing thoughts and pressured speech (for the person with autism who doesn't speak, or has limited speech, this may be increased intensity in singing, babbling, or humming).

Please know that I have yet to meet someone with autism who has not experienced some degree of clinical depression – it's that common. If it's going to surface, it will likely develop at the onset of adolescence (ages ten through thirteen), and at the time when a young person becomes painfully aware – or is made to feel painfully aware – of their differences. This is the age at which, more than ever, young people are defining their own individuality and are very conscious of how others present themselves. In my work as a consultant, more often than not the person who is challenging to support is discovered to have bipolar disorder – even in young children.

Consult a psychiatrist once you've captured the above information. As much as they would like to, psychiatrists rarely have time to review extensive volumes of documentation. I advise drawing up a *one-page*, bullet-point document organizing the information if it makes sense given what you know to be true about the person. (Be certain to include a separate bullet statement addressing any known cycles, and family history.) If it doesn't make sense for the person you know and care about, be prepared to express why. Also provide a brief synopsis of previous diagnoses and medications tried.

My greatest challenge as an autism consultant is in convincing people (parents, professionals, and psychiatrists) that bipolar disorder may be a very real possibility for an individual with autism. Sometimes parents and caregivers are so caught up in the daily activities of life that it is difficult for them to see the forest for the trees until the situation reaches an unbearable point of crisis. It is so very important to take aggressive action in exploring someone's mental health *before* this happens. It only stresses everyone concerned, and has taken its toll on more than a few marriages. In spite of implementing all the good and kind person-centered philosophies we've been discussing, all attempts to support someone with autism and mental illness *will be* stymied at every turn by the manifestation of the illness's symptoms unless the issues are addressed. What I see with rampant frequency are situations involving big teenage boys and young men with autism who are out of control, and for whom psychiatric hospitalization, or out-of-school, out-of-home, out-of-state placements are being sought. In all instances, the young men have had bipolar disorder that has been undiagnosed or inappropriately clinically supported. These men are testament to why behavior and other treatment plans, antipsychotic medications, psychiatric hospitalizations and other placements are unsuccessful. Such situations are preventable, but know that the longer the needle plays on the record, the deeper the groove becomes.

Educate yourself about current best practices in clinically supporting mood disorders. Antipsychotics are not best practice treatment. Although they are the drugs of choice by many psychiatrists, they will only slow down the person with mania, making them appear "drugged" and lethargic, more manageable and perhaps seemingly more compliant. What occurs is that the true diagnosis has been muddied or masked; it still exists, it just doesn't surface through the murk as readily. (On occasion, a very short-term, time-limited antipsychotic *in conjunction with* a mood stabilizing medication has been helpful in supporting the acute phase until that portion of the bipolar experience subsides.)

Giving someone in the depression phase of bipolar disorder an antidepressant may be likened to pouring gasoline on fire, and will generally propel him or her into full-blown mania. Learn about mood stabilizing medications that may help someone to feel balanced and in the driver's seat once more. Three such medications are Lithium, Depakote and Tegretol. Depakote and Tegretol are anticonvulsants, but were discovered to have mood stabilizing effects when given at higher doses to folks with seizure disorders. When a mood stabilizer is ineffective in treating someone with bipolar disorder, it is usually because the trial wasn't long enough, or the dosage wasn't high enough to boost the person's blood level to a therapeutic range for the drug's use *as a mood stabilizer* — not an anticonvulsant. Laboratories that process medication blood levels will indicate a standard range, but this range is usually not high enough for the drug's use as a mood stabilizer. Ask the psychiatrist what he or she projects for the person who is struggling. Do they see the premise and rationale for mood disorder? If not, respectfully request that they explain. Why are they prescribing the medications they prescribe? What would they consider to be an ideal therapeutic blood level for this person, and why? What are the side effects to be mindful of? Are there any contraindications (adverse reactions) with any other medications the person is currently taking?

Some people able to self-report may be opposed to taking medication, or may be physically unable to sustain medication without significant physical side effects. These folks may wish to explore alternatives such as St John's Wort (for depression) and other natural supplements in addition to the wellness activities discussed. Above all, please strive to understand the person's inner struggle, and recognize and acknowledge any of their coping successes. For example, I have known people who will refuse to eat with their families because they have enough foresight to know the noise, visual stimuli, and social interactions could set them off. Similarly, one gentleman would, at times, insist on eating from paper cups and plates because he foresaw the potential to throw them. Another young man insisted upon occupying his hands so he would be less likely to strike others. These folks did not want to do harm, and were coping the very best way they knew how. How such behavior is interpreted, though, is a matter of sensitive objectivity.

We've already discussed the concept of safety in sameness and comfort in what is familiar as it relates to needing to feel in control. As a child, I grew up in a house from which the high school was visible on a hill in the distance. While peers were worried about childish concerns like Martians invading their backyards, I feared the Martians *and* wondered how I'd ever know how to catch the bus in order to get to the high school years before it was ever a consideration. There is so much about the big world that may seem out of control that such perceptions can appear to become heightened, exaggerated or blown out of proportion for the person with autism. Many folks torture themselves similarly by agonizing over inexorable detail, particularly with regard to future changes or impeding events. Anxiety also manifests severely when one is the focus of anger or sharp words. Even if such wrath is not directed at the person, the anxiety will escalate as well as if it had been. The persistence of dark mood may then permeate the hour, morning, rest of the day or into the following day. It may lead to the manifestation of hypersensitive behavior, being unable to calm, focus and rest, or repeated requests for confirmation. Many of the philosophies and recommendations I've suggested are designed to concurrently provide control while serving to quell anxiety, and have proven helpful for many.

Know, too, the great potential for folks with autism to experience Post Traumatic Stress Disorder (PTSD). The symptoms may share commonalities with those of depression, but added symptoms may include: nightmares, night sweats or other sleep complaints; unusual sexual behavior (reenactments of sexual abuse) or the perpetration of sexual behavior upon others; clinginess or general fearfulness; withdrawal from social activity; "flashback" experiences (or "zoning out" by staring into space) triggered by people, places, visuals, and smells; physically or verbally "replaying" past events, or dwelling upon discussion of such; bedwetting; heightened anxiety; constant seeking of assurances; feeling unsafe or unprotected in familiar environments, or vehemently refusing to be in a certain environment; complaints of feeling physically or sexually "dirty," and frequently bathing; illustrating a past experience through writing, art or music; and being hypervigilant (being "on guard" or easily startled).

In considering PTSD, remember that we are talking about caring for and supporting exquisitely sensitive beings who may internalize and agonize over minute detail. A gentle and respectful therapist, knowledgeable about PTSD, will allow the person to share what they choose to as it comes in the environment most comfortable for that person (that doesn't mean a doctor's office!), without pressing for information. Above all else, someone with PTSD needs an ally; someone in whom they can confide unconditionally and without fear of reprisal.

It is not enough, though, to understand mental health issues in persons with different ways of being if those individuals are not partners in understanding their own experience. This is important in order for folks to be strong self-advocates. We are all ultimately temporary in the lives of the people we know and care about. Therefore it is very important that each individual has self-knowledge of one's own experience, and a way to communicate it. Social stories (adapted to suit the person) are one good way of communicating information about mental health, and I suggest that analogies be used and practiced with each person. Examples may include a pictorial scale of mood or wellness for each day indicated by the intensity of expression on a sequence of illustrated faces. Perhaps consider pictorially likening mood swings to hills and valleys, a roller-coaster ride, the ebb and flow of ocean tides, the rise and fall of a thermometer's mercury, or maybe use the car analogy (successful with one young man who accurately related where he was "sitting" in the hypothetical car depending upon his experience). Confidentiality and privacy are, naturally, paramount in when and where such discussions take place, and it is crucial that caregivers protect an individual's rights to personal disclosure.

Finally, the simplest of sentiments: true love conquers all. When consulting in support of someone with autism in adolescence and older, I usually ask the question, "Who do you love?" or "Who do you want to love?" It is a subtle way of addressing someone's sexuality, often disregarded in supporting others with differences, but it also establishes a hope. Love alone is not enough, *but* anytime I have ever seen anyone lifted out of depression, or better poised to proactively progress in life, it has been because of a relationship that has been meaningful for the person. It may not necessarily be a romantic relationship, but may be a true and genuine friendship of unconditional, mutual trust and acceptance.

Guiding Principles – Mental Health

- Mental illness is an equal-opportunity offender – it does not distinguish between brains

- Mental health issues are not the person's fault; their actions are not of their volition

- Many people with autism are misdiagnosed or undiagnosed with mental health issues

- Rule out the potential for mood disorder by understanding symptomology – not by describing "behaviors"

- Mood disorders may manifest differently in persons with autism

- Family history and the presence of cycles impact one's vulnerability to mental health issues

- You don't medicate autism

- Unless the mental health issue is properly identified and supported, all our other efforts will be unsuccessful

- Anxiety and post traumatic stress disorder are commonplace for people with an autistic experience

- Self-knowledge and self-advocacy are of high importance

- True love conquers all

Chapter 7

My Self-Revelation

One of this book's themes has been that we are all more alike than different. As part of my workshop intended to demystify autism, I invite participants to reflect upon those things that they know to be true about themselves – that others might consider eccentric or idiosyncratic – but which work for them. Women in the audience are usually the first to open up, and as the discussion flows I joke about how cleansing it is to relieve ourselves of these long-held burdens. The men take a bit more coaxing, but it is intriguing when they do share information because males are four times more likely than females to be autistic. That's why the book *Men are from Mars, Women are from Venus* has been so popular. If I may generalize for a moment, a chief female complaint about men is that they are often oblivious to subtle nuances, hints, and innuendo in women's conversational intonation and body language. Men generally don't do well trying to decipher such signals; they need to be hit over the head with concrete and direct information (remember, say what you mean and mean what you say?).

Some audience anecdotes include rigidity in schedules and personal environments, or needing to execute activities in a certain set procedure. Other universal experiences involve temporary "brain fades" many of us have had, like "gray" time while driving: that is, driving from point A to point B, and upon arrival at point B, having no recollection of the drive. A similar experience involves needing to deviate from one's typical driving route to drop something or someone off, or pick up something or someone – and ending up going the regular way, and having to backtrack once the mistake is realized. Additionally, many of us have also had the maddening experience of being unable to recall the name of someone we know when we meet them unexpectedly or out of environmental context.

Thus far, I've been suggestive but deliberately evasive with regard to my own experience. This is because I wanted the reader to focus on the message first, and not be distracted with deconstructing my differences. I've always been aware of the differences but, until fairly recently, I was without a framework to explain them. As a result, I've often been exasperated, frustrated and depressed by my "disconnection" from others, despite my concerted efforts to fit in.

It was my sweet friend Jasmine Lee O'Neill who first suggested that Asperger's Syndrome might make sense for me. I had some idea about autism, but my knowledge was mostly stereotypical information generated by the media. Befriending Jasmine and fellow artist Barbara Moran served to shatter those stereotypes and open my thinking to other possibilities. I knew I wasn't autistic, but, in talking with my friends, I also knew I had a lot in common with them and their respective life experiences. Reading the clinical definition of Asperger's Syndrome (one of autism's cousins) seemed to make more sense, particularly as I reflected upon my childhood and adolescence. One day, I sat at my computer and developed a list of all the things I knew to be true about myself that were Asperger's or autistic-like. The list was a substantial one, and I will relate much of it here in autobiographical format.

I believe that as a child I had no known developmental delays (one criterion for Asperger's), but was socially withdrawn. Curiously, I recently watched some old home movies taken of me at about age three. In my objective viewing as an adult, what I saw was a small boy with a somewhat melancholy or confused expression who is more interested in playing in the water of a birdbath than in interacting socially. In one instance, another child races toward me from across a lawn, and I appear to reciprocate; but instead of physically connecting with or embracing the other child, I continue running directly past the (bewildered) kid.

In later years, and before I knew what Asperger's was, I would use the phrase "socially retarded" to describe myself. As a young boy I was beyond shy, and often stoically serious. I was also intensely emotionally sensitive, and could burst into tears despairing over the lyrics of Peter, Paul and Mary's "Where Have all the Flowers Gone?" or "Puff, the Magic Dragon." (Both songs are about irreversible change.) Once, I was removed from church because I could not control my weeping. Unbeknown to anyone else, I had been staring at a stained glass window of the crucifixion, and was grieving for the pain Christ must have experienced.

When my social interactions involved my controlling, directing and participating in reenacting scenes from *The Wizard of Oz*, I experienced social and creative success. On any other occasion, I floundered miserably, being unable or uncertain about how to proceed. Suffice it to say, I stink at making small talk. I remember quite clearly standing on the playground at first grade recess, watching the other children run and play and having *no clue* as to what it was I was supposed to be doing. Not that I minded. Quite frankly, if it didn't involve Oz, I was disinterested. That's the difference between being shy and being Asperger's. Secretly, the shy child desperately wants to be invited to participate; I could not have cared less. When I was younger, other children were essentially moving objects to me. Conversely, as an adult, I have always marveled at how children previously unknown to one another will naturally gravitate to each other and initiate sustained play. I find the mechanics of this phenomenon fascinating.

The Wizard of Oz sustained me socially during the mid to late 1960s. The annual television airings of the movie were *the* defining childhood event in those days, and to have an aficionado in their midst was appealing for several neighborhood children as I controlled our play. Even the trauma of leaving home to attend kindergarten was softened when my teacher rolled out a yellow brick road path so that the mothers who accompanied us first-day students to school could find their way to the principal's office. The same teacher also played excerpts from the movie soundtrack recording during rest times. Sporadic playdates in the homes of other children pivoted upon my ability to quickly discern any Oz items in the house, which then became the focus.

While *The Wizard of Oz* was an acceptable and encouraged playtime subject, in time I reached an age at which my peers outgrew it while I held fast. My interest remained constant at a time when other children's interests became "flavor of the week" dynamic. During this transition, my poor grandmother graciously tolerated endless telephone conversations during which I released encyclopedic information about Oz pseudonyms, statistics and other minutiae. Of course my intense "childish" interest coupled with my physical lack of coordination made me ripe for becoming a target of peer abuse as I grew. This is precisely what transpired.

One kid in particular made me his personal whipping boy for about six years, from grades four through nine. (Fortunately, by tenth grade high school, people seemed to have matured beyond such taunting for the most part.) At every opportunity, he would publicly humiliate and embarrass me; and privately, he would physically strike me to elicit a reaction, although I never did react outwardly. Soon others followed, and by junior high school and high school, I was definitely odd man out.

Once in seventh grade homeroom, a boy suddenly stood up and began to pummel me for no reason obvious to me. I was instantly caught up in what was, for all intent and purposes, a one-sided fistfight (the classroom teacher was outside at the end of the hall, socializing). Terrified, and never having been in such a violent situation, I didn't know how to react. Classmates were cheering and jeering us on. In between trying to push the boy off me, I laughed, as though

I wasn't taking it seriously; as though the whole thing were a joke put on for show. Eventually I broke free, a trembling, nervous wreck, and shot out into the hall to find the teacher, who was oblivious and unconcerned with the matter. The incident set a regrettable precedent. I was now a superlatively easy target for physical abuse, even from the boys who weren't considered tough at all.

Gym class and the lunchroom – culprits in social horror for most folks with Asperger's – were unbearable. Once, in gym class, I got hit in the groin with a volleyball. I wasn't hit hard so it didn't really hurt but felt numb. I didn't know how to react in order to "perform" for what the class expected of a guy in that unenviable circumstance. Should I over-react, grab my crotch and howl, which would have elicited more laughter, or should I just ignore it? I made a split-second decision and opted for the latter, but was damned either way. My non-reaction prompted comments about there not being anything there to injure. Of course I was also one of those unfortunates always to be picked last when choosing sides. On another occasion, I miraculously scored a touchdown during a football game. After reaching the goal line, the other kids started yelling at me to "spike" the ball. I didn't know what that was or what it looked like until one boy demonstrated. I reenacted it with mock enthusiasm. Similarly, I never understood school pep rallies, and dreaded attending them simply because I didn't know their purpose. I didn't feel anything, but went along with it because the kids who opted out were considered underachievers, persons without school spirit, or drug users, and were sent to the library to linger for the duration.

The high-school cafeteria was horrific because of the lengthy unstructured time in a crowded, noisy environment. When my family temporarily moved to a new school district, the homeroom teacher mercifully told another boy to make sure I had a place to sit in the lunchroom. Fortunately, the boy complied but, as usual, I was painfully flat and awkward when interacting with him and his friends. I eventually said little to nothing and ate in silence. One day, I walked into the lunchroom to find our table commandeered by all new faces. I panicked. What had happened? The assigned period hadn't changed. What had occurred was that the group I sat with changed tables without telling me in an effort to lose me. Unfortunately for them, I found them. Other years, I sought out anyone at all to sit with – even younger siblings of classmates; not because I was interested in socializing, but for protection against being perceived as different. Finally, I gave up, accepted my fate and sat alone with my face in a book (and became nearsighted for doing so). Toward the end of high school, I even eventually stopped taking the bus – yet *another* unstructured environment – and walked the several miles home to avoid public humiliations by kids who would catcall or mimic my speech and body language.

In hindsight, I know now that, in addition to depression, I suffered Post Traumatic Stress Disorder (PTSD) because of these experiences. This manifested itself in bed-wetting into adolescence, feigning illness to avoid school attendance, withdrawal, nightmares, and anxiety about being in the general school environment. The nightmares lingered far beyond high school into adulthood. But as my life began to change in positive directions, I sought to assert control over the experience. I was a decent person with something of value to contribute, but my self-esteem had nearly been stripped bare. (Even today, it is very difficult for me to accept compliments because of feeling unworthy of them.) I have always had powerful dreams, and have sometimes received meaningful information in dreams. My PTSD resolved itself in a dream one night. In the dream, my antagonists were seated around a large table. I stood behind them, and proceeded to circle the table, leaning forward to kiss each one on the cheek in an act of forgiveness. Upon awakening, I was healed and never again plagued by the haunting nightmares of abuse.

I am the oldest of four boys (being oldest seems to be a trend in guys with Asperger's), which allowed me to hold authority over my younger brothers. From ages six to sixteen, I also grew up in a house across the street from a very active playground. I'm sure that I caused my brothers much embarrassment because of rumors about my Oz passion and bizarre behavior. My absence at the playground was glaringly conspicuous to some who queried my brothers about it; and unnoticed by those who didn't realize my brothers even had an older sibling. This resurfaced when a junior high school teacher who lived in the neighborhood once asked in class, "Didn't you used to be *weird?*" As I became more stigmatized, I exerted more control over my brothers and, at times, could become violently insistent. Mostly, I either had no friends, had age-inappropriate friendships (meaning I was drawn to interacting with kids younger than I was whom I could impress, control and manipulate, and who were still interested in the same things as me; or I was friendly with adults who found me intriguing and indulged my interests), or I had transient friendships that grew fruitless and dissipated because there wasn't enough to sustain them.

As mentioned, I spent inordinate amounts of time in my room, which was arranged rather exactingly. On walks through the nearby woods, I would gather appealing leaves, ferns and rocks and mount elaborate displays on my dresser top, replete with identification placards. I became infuriated when anyone would disturb the precise arrangement of my museum-like presentations, but with three younger brothers this occurred with outrageous frequency. I was fascinated by Walt Disney's films and developed plans for my own animated films, painstakingly making "flip book" drawings to replicate animation sequences. I went through a period in which I adopted very formal language, spelling words like "colour" and "favourite" the English way, announcing that I would properly address my parents as "Mother" and "Father," and using words such as "to and fro" instead of "back and forth." I smiled with recognition when reading the anecdote in Becky Moyes' book, *Incorporating Social Skills in the Classroom*, about the boy who, at the dinner table, asked his mother for more "game," referencing that meal's meat.

On several occasions, I spent time during summers at the New Jersey beach house of my godparents. My godmother, presumably aware of my social aloofness, once sought to connect me with the similarly aged grandson of the woman next door, but the duration of the "connection" lasted only an hour or two one afternoon. What did make spending time at the shore appealing was that my godparents had several old Oz books in the house. This was at a time when my passion for Oz was at its most intense, and I spent much time pouring over the books, taking in their aged, musty scent, and reveling in revisiting the storylines and being transported to Oz. I knew that my godparents must have other Oz books at their home north of the shore, because one of my earliest childhood memories was of wandering alone upstairs in that house, and coming upon a box of books designated as library donations. The second floor of their substantial home had rows of built-in bookcases filled, floor to ceiling, and with sometimes more than one edition of the same book. On top of the box was the 1939 movie edition of *The Wizard of Oz*, which I vividly remember discovering. I begged and nagged my godmother to take me back to the house, too embarrassed to explain that I wanted to search for more Oz books. It must have been a long drive because she was hesitant, where ordinarily she would spoil and accommodate me. I eventually wore her down, and we made the trip. One of her sons (then twenty-something) had had the house to himself, and, upon our arrival, she exclaimed aloud that the house was a mess. I agreed that it was, and she quite unexpectedly laid into me, yelling that I must have overheard her concerns about him taking care of the place and that was the only reason why I wanted to come to the house – to check up on him. Frustrated, she said, "This is why you don't have any friends, Billy!" I burst into tears as she folded me in her arms, apologizing. I was too ashamed to admit that the truth was that I loved the house, and was anxious to explore it for more Oz books.

There were a few things that saved me from complete social extinction. Most prominent was that I was inordinately artistically gifted as a child. I have always been drawn to detail, and can recollect miniscule detail going back to infancy. I've also always been a visual thinker and learner because I *think* in constant streams of visual imagery. When engaged in conversation, I see, visually, the person and environment around us *and* I see the images of our discussion in my mind. It's only recently that I've learned that most people don't think this way, which is a bit disconcerting, and begs the question: What's in there then? Empty blackness? Similarly, as a child, I especially enjoyed bedtime because that was when I was best able to entertain myself by selectively replaying mind movies, as easily as you remove a favorite book from its shelf.

It's curious, but I've found that guys with Asperger's fall at either end of a spectrum. There are the mathematical wizards, adept at crunching numbers and deciphering computers and other mechanical devices without regard for instruction manuals; and then there are the poets, musicians, actors and artists at the other end. Given my relationship with numbers (we maintain a polite distance now), I definitely lean toward the opposite, creative end of the continuum.

I recall first being made aware of my artistic gift when, in kindergarten, we each were asked to fill a large creamy sheet of manila paper with a crayoned self-portrait. Of course I did as I was told and, oblivious of the others, went about the task of creating an image of a boy with a black crew cut and green eyes. I didn't realize my drawing was any different from anyone else's until I suddenly realized that the *entire* class *and* the teacher were crowded around me, looking at my picture! (I had no idea how long they had been there and was unaware of the fuss that must have been communicated about my drawing.)

On another occasion in first grade, we were asked to draw a picture of ourselves with our pets. I began to draw my childhood dog, but the dog I drew turned out to look more like Dorothy's dog, Toto. So I naturally inserted Dorothy frolicking alongside Toto, the misinterpretation of which raised concerns about my sexual identity.

Also at an early age (three and up), I was fascinated with the paper engineering of pop-up books, and other similar activity books. In trying to replicate the devices I had carefully observed in books in department stores or in a neighbor's home, I recall investing much time in creating elaborate books of my own with hidden panels or tabs, fold-out areas that revealed a hidden image through a peephole, three-dimensional wings on a bird, and incorporating a collage of cutouts clipped from a favorite picture book. In 1968, Random House issued an exquisitely rendered set of pop-up books of classic tales. *The Wizard of Oz* was the first title in the series, and I acquired this and a number of other titles in the set (*Alice in Wonderland, Pinocchio, Snow White*). Between the ages of about six and eight, I immersed myself in studying the books, completely intrigued by the seamless façade that concealed their complex construction between the pages. I began to deconstruct the books (starting with *Oz*, of course) and replicate them in copies of my own – precisely rendered in full color, and articulated exactingly and authentic to the originals. I spent hours and hours, and weekends and entire summers alone in my room deep in my work. When I wasn't duplicating the pop-ups, then I was drawing the Oz characters over and over again. I didn't understand the reaction, though, when I would take my pop-up replicas to school or Sunday school class to show teachers who were astounded and disbelieving. I took my talent for granted because it was a natural part of who I was.

The talent also saved me socially at times. Teachers would highlight my work, or ask me to effect room decor. Children who would otherwise seek to denigrate me would be awestruck and deceptively cordial when the time came to do something creative in class, and I welcomed their "friendship." I began taking commissions for artwork from adults when I was twelve. For a time, I was even able to stay indoors during recess in order to draw under the guidance of a doting art teacher.

Also, as a child and adolescent, people found me physically attractive. As a child I was unconcerned with it, and as a teenager I was possessed of such woefully poor self-esteem that I welcomed the compliments when they came, but privately was entirely self-deprecating. However, when people laud your talent and appearance as superior to others, what they're also doing is making concessions for atypical or eccentric behavior. We witness this phenomenon regularly in the behavior of sports figures and other celebrities whose status has been elevated to exaggerated proportions. In order to continue to meet others' expectations, I have always been overly fastidious about my personal grooming. I think a lot of my early anti-social behavior was "masked" because of my giftedness, or because I "passed" well enough that I didn't reveal a lot of my struggles to my parents since I was too embarrassed to confess that I was different. To a great extent, Asperger's Syndrome is an invisible disability for those individuals who appear so highly skilled, but who have limitations that can exceed others' expectations (and, frustratingly, their own).

The final thing that sustained me was a sense of purpose in life. From a very young age, I've had an intangible awareness that someday people would know who I was because of what I had to offer. I was never sure when or how it would happen, but I always carried with me this sense of having been "recognized" for a greater purpose. I've also always felt that someone or something was watching over me, protecting me, and, at times, rescuing me from uncertain or unwise predicaments. I was first cognizant of it when, as a toddler, I slipped under the water just off shore of a beach on a lake. My family was sitting at the water's edge but apparently didn't see what happened quickly enough. I remember calling for help (either verbally or in my thoughts), and was instantly supported within a bubble that enclosed my head such that I could breathe until I was pulled from the water.

The next time I sensed my protective predestiny was when an inner voice dissuaded me from taking my own life at the age of sixteen. Alone in the house, I contemplated my father's old straight razor and imagined the sensation of the blood slowly seeping from my body as I drifted away. I am most grateful that I didn't take my life, but it should be recognized that suicide among people with Asperger's is not uncommon because of the great propensity for depression, as we've discussed. However, on numerous occasions I have been very fortunate; and it's been more than just luck or coincidence. There have been things I've done or became engaged in that, if discovered, would have surely branded me and taken my life in different directions.

There reached a time, though, when my parents determined that they needed to intervene. At twelve years old and on the verge of transitioning to junior high school, my parents and I entered into what seemed like nightly "talks." As I neared adolescence, they were concerned about how my interest in *The Wizard of Oz* would be perceived by my peers, especially if any were to be invited home to my room, in which I had a small but substantial collection of memorabilia. What they didn't know was that it was too late. The talks were a mostly one-sided discussion about setting my Oz things aside (though, mercifully not disposing of them) in favor of striving to become more sociable in school through participating in after-school clubs or sports. What I recall of the talks was me sitting there, sobbing and grieving for the loss of something that was an integral part of who I was. Amidst the tears, I struggled with what seemed to be an inconceivable betrayal: how is it that, in prior years, my passion was valued and encouraged, but was now something to conceal? I couldn't comprehend the rationale, but, in hindsight, I understand that my parents (who were quite young parents) were trying to do their best. What I can tell you, though, is that it was the only time in my life that my heart has been broken. No *person* could ever make me feel the hurt I experienced at that time. People disappoint; passions never do. If, in some twisted, other-world logic, my parents had suggested I elect to have my right hand surgically removed in concession for keeping my Oz things near to me always, I would have opted for the surgery without missing a beat — it meant that much. What happened, though, was that, while my passion for Oz was temporarily suppressed, other interests nearly as intense surfaced to take its place; and we were back to square one. The compromise was that I could keep my Oz things in the attic (with regular visiting privileges), but must enroll in a school activity, preferably a sport.

I reluctantly signed up for what seemed like the sport least likely to create more undue humiliation – cross-country running. The activity was not at all social for me, but I didn't mind the running so much because it was a solitary activity. I just didn't have the stamina to run for miles as many of the others could, and usually came in last. This was compounded when the coach recorded our time and number status aloud upon completing the course. We would be given both upon coming in, and were expected to relay the information when our number was called. Once, the coach made a very specific statement about making sure we listened carefully so that he could make the notations correctly and expeditiously. I remember mentally *telling* myself to ensure I paid attention when my time came, but somehow my thoughts were elsewhere when my number was called, which prompted many smirks, rolled eyes and shaking heads. Fortunately, the following summer I suffered a third-degree ankle sprain in my first and only encounter with a skateboard; cross-country was out of the question for the new school year.

For a time, I went through a period of inappropriately silly behavior. In junior high school, there were a couple of girls who would make faces or say things to me while the teacher wasn't looking. That would set me off and I would giggle uncontrollably, embarrassing myself and garnering stares from classmates. Why I never got kicked out of class I'll never know; I certainly should have been. I just could not regain composure, and was often very upset about it afterwards.

I have always "passed" by incorporating bits of dialogue from favorite films in my everyday speech. Often, this has been paired with replicating a character's body language as well. It is very subtle and, unless you know me intimately, it is undetectable. It is a crutch that I've employed, particularly in settings that are socially awkward and uncomfortable. Projecting a persona has always made sense, especially when I've wanted to be anyone other than myself. I often think that I don't really have my own personality; I'm made up of bits and pieces of other people. When I see or hear someone do something I like, I pluck it and add it to my bag of tricks. When appropriate, I simply conjure it back up and put it out. In time, I collected jokes and comedic observations too, many of which I used for years. But my humor was usually witheringly sarcastic and biting. I sought to inflict pain because I had endured so much myself. In later years, I could misjudge a social situation so that my use of humor was totally inappropriate, or I would receive laughs in reaction to something I said in all seriousness (which often still occurs).

I still use "movie talk," so you can imagine my pleasant surprise to learn that many kids with Asperger's do this too – I thought I was alone. I'm often "in a movie," even when I'm alone or driving in the car. I project a cool, assured persona by assuming dialogue and traits that I've stowed away in my repertoire. On other occasions, however, I have unwittingly assumed personality traits of others by osmosis of sorts, particularly persons who have supervised me in an employment setting. This is problematic if they have attitudes that do not reflect my own.

I was able to parlay my adept ability to "act" into legitimate opportunities in high-school productions. The first dramatic part I auditioned for, though, I overacted, giving an exaggerated and clichéd reading. Needless to say I didn't get that part, but later I got the lead role of a young boy who was psychologically disturbed by doing my best Tony Perkins/*Psycho* imitation. I was ultimately not a very successful actor; I was a mimic without an emotional reserve on which to draw, as any good actor would do. Acting was an opportunity to become someone else and emote. My facial affect was typically so flat that my mother said, "I think if you'd ever smile your face would crack!" As I was musically inclined and could sing (as a child I could play by ear on a keyboard a song I had just heard on the radio), I also got the leads in high-school musicals. This abetted both my self-esteem and social standing, as you might imagine, and my senior year of school was largely tolerable and, at times, really enjoyable.

Academically, I did poorly in math and science courses, falling well behind the classes I should have been taking at my grade level, and ending up repeating an algebra course. Although I'm articulate, I've never been intelligent in a traditional sense and, like many others, "test" poorly (my SAT scores were deplorable). Socially, I was expanding and had become somewhat accepted. I had a clique of sorts through my acting colleagues, and engaged in more social activities after school. I was even invited to illustrate the cover of our yearbook. Then, I was fascinated with the concept of subliminal suggestion, one tactic used by advertisers at the time whereby a nearly invisible web of words like "sex" was imperceptibly embedded over photo images in an advertisement. So, in executing the cover illustration of an eagle, our mascot, chiseling the cornerstone of our school, I hid the word "sex" (among others) dozens of times throughout the drawing. No one ever knew until now.

I still ran the risk of being taken advantage of because of wanting to fit in. This is typical of many folks with Asperger's. We don't question what people tell us to do, we just do it because they said so. One friend got me to take her to an expensive seafood restaurant once a week, even though I had to withdraw money from my rapidly depleting savings account in order to do it. Other times I got involved in some destructive vandalism because of just wanting to fit in with a group, not unlike any number of teenagers.

Like my thoughts on pep rallies, I didn't understand the excitement and formality surrounding high-school graduation, but went through the paces nonetheless. (I was glad to get it over with, and didn't bother participating in college graduation when the time came.) Before the end of my senior year, I enrolled in a nearby college known for its art program. I wasn't sure that pursuing an art career was necessarily something I wanted to do. My artistic ability wasn't really an interest so much as something I could do well. Given my success in high-school acting, I thought an entertainment career was a more glamorous aspiration. My parents were supportive, but insistent that I have a degree to "fall back on," so I majored in art education, which meant I'd receive a teaching certificate.

After initially commuting to school, I was able to get a placement in an on-campus dormitory. In an unlikely pairing, my first college roommate was an athlete with brash, coarse friends who would hang out in our room, which I disliked for the lack of privacy. Here, too, I was odd man out and my flat affect didn't exactly ingratiate me. I didn't know that when another guy passes you in the hallway and silently nods his head, that is the same as communicating "Hi, how's it going, what's up?" So, I didn't react after making eye contact and kept moving, staring straight ahead. This quickly labeled me as cold and aloof, and I became the subject of talk. Some passive-aggressive behavior began to transpire during my roommate's gatherings in our room. I had decorated my half of the room with movie posters saved from a part-time job as a theatre usher. Some of them gradually fell into "disrepair" in my absence, as did my alarm clock, which became increasingly chipped and cracked until it was unusable. Of course I kept silent about all of this, which was the same as giving consent to perpetuate it.

Socially, I fell back into my need to pair up with anyone in order to appear normal, regardless of whether there existed genuine investment on my part or theirs. I bought people from class dinner off campus so I wouldn't have to eat alone in the school cafeteria. On another occasion, a long weekend on campus, I had made plans to go to a football game with an acquaintance in my dormitory. I had no interest in the game; it was a ploy to fill a void of time. The morning before the game, I went to his room to confirm our plans, and discovered him asleep and surrounded by family and relatives talking in hushed tones while he rested. I stood in the doorway and called his name until he awakened. I asked my question, received his groggy, brief response and left, oblivious to the rudeness of my behavior. Later, when he addressed my rudeness, I was affronted and distanced myself from him thereafter. Fortunately, I did have a few connections in people that I knew from high school. But every time I thought I was fitting in, I ended up being excluded, overlooked or forgotten when it came to time for group activities. It was distressing and maddening, and I could never understand it.

I became rather slovenly, not caring about clean sheets or clothes, and skipping 8:00 am classes in order to sleep in. Thank goodness I was a talented art major. I could complete assignments quickly and effortlessly, and received glowing recognition for my work from peers and professors. Otherwise I continued to flounder with math, biology, social science, and history courses, again needing to repeat an algebra course that I just barely passed the second time. My study skills were weak. I was disinterested in making the time to study as I needed to, and, when I did, the material was unable to hold my interest as I was distracted by more personally interesting things. If I can't make a "picture" of it I can't retain it.

I was able to make a connection with another guy in my art classes who I found humorous and gregarious – traits that have always been appealing to me in others because of my own lack of humor and outgoingness. (I still cannot understand how many people watch sitcom TV programs every evening and laugh hard and out loud.) We became roommates for the second half of the year. Being an art colleague, my friend was creative and uninhibited. He seemed accepting of my sarcastic edge and was admiring of my talent. It was at this time that a remake of the movie *Cat People* was released, and we both got caught up in the concept of shape shifting to other forms. For a period of time, when in our dorm room, I became a black panther, leaping to and from my bunkbed top, and pouncing with feline precision to position myself on our radiator. My recounting an especially vivid dream about stalking about on campus in my panther persona validated this behavior. Not that my roommate minded; he was enamored of *The Incredible Hulk*, and would periodically metamorphosis into a massive monster.

After my first year, I switched schools for personal reasons (which I'll discuss later), and commuted from a new living arrangement. This suited me well because I had much less unstructured free time, except for lengthy gaps between some classes. I was not obligated to assume any false pretenses or feign investment in anyone at all. I basically kept to myself, ate lunch in my car, and pored over ancient periodicals in the library's archives. (Liane Holliday Willey's book, *Pretending to be Normal*, offers some great tips for would-be college students, and addresses such downtime issues.) Otherwise, getting around campus could be problematic. This pertained especially to classes that I only had once or twice a week. I had difficulty finding certain buildings, or – once inside the buildings – finding my way to the classrooms. This would cause me to panic or feel disoriented. I essentially got around by "feeling" my way out; having a murky sense of where I needed to be, and moving in that general direction until things became more familiar, like identifying markers on a wooded trail. (In school, I had similar difficulty remembering where my locker was located, or using its combination.)

This sense of disorientation also relates to driving. I have done some rather reckless things while driving that made sense to me at the time because of my own logic in knowing I needed to get from here to there, such as making a U-turn across a median strip in a four-way highway. I have come to understand that I need to insist upon very explicit and detailed driving directions *to and from* my destination, complete with exact street names and landmarks. Otherwise I can become horribly confused and panic stricken, totally unhinged by the time I finally arrive. Years later, I had the worst driving experience of all, maneuvering my way around downtown Philadelphia, parking in a completely disorienting garage, and finding my way to a hotel meeting room, accessible by only one of a pair of elevators (the other elevator led to completely different floors). By the time I reached the meeting, I was significantly late, totally undone, drenched in perspiration, and numb and oblivious to the conversation. Upon leaving, I was convinced that my car had been stolen because it was not where I carefully noted it had been parked. It took two attendants to lead me to my car, parked right where I had left it.

Upon graduating from college with an art education teaching degree, I was most fortunate to secure my first job in the school district where I had done my intern student teaching. Teaching elementary age school children was great fun because I so related to their naive sense of wonder and joy in exploration and discovery of self-expression through art. I could be wildly flamboyant in making a point, standing on my desk top or demonstrating a technique while singing to contain their attention – and they accepted it unconditionally, laughing, smiling and enjoying themselves. I was also *in control* of up to thirty little people for six to eight sessions a day. This is why a number of people with Asperger's make good instructors or university professors. In addition to the control issue, you are the center of positive attention predicated upon the good things you have to offer (builds self-esteem). There is a regimented schedule, and you are required to prepare lesson plan outlines for each class.

I flourished in the classroom and garnered much peer praise for my enthusiastic contribution. But in the staff room, I was as hopelessly inadequate as I had been during any other unstructured time in my own school career, speaking only when spoken to. One teacher who took a liking to me invited me to a small dinner gathering in his home. My persona projected coolness and reserve, and when one of the guests monopolized the conversation I caused someone to spit their drink when I deadpanned, "I'm afraid I've been ignorant to everything you've been talking about." I didn't mean to be rude. I was being honest and direct, but my remark brought things to a temporary standstill.

The following school year saw the job curtailed to part time, which I supplemented by working in a record store. The environment of the record store was rather bourgeois and of a culture that clashed with mine. I was attracted to the position because I saw potential to create ingenious displays of publicity posters and other materials. I was not well accepted by the other employees, and banned from using the cash register after too many avoidable errors. Once, though, a group of my co-workers invited me to join them at the movies, probably as a lark. I hesitantly kept the date, and when I showed up there were whispers of disbelief.

Afterwards, my expressed misunderstanding of the movie's plot provided the outlet for them to release their pent-up laughter.

After my second year of teaching, the position was cut back to one day a week, and it was no longer feasible for me to stay on. The employment I could find closest to teaching was in human services, providing direct care to people with learning differences living in community homes. I could relate well to others who had been perceived as different and persecuted for it. Because the work setting was homelike, I contended with others who played TVs and radios incessantly, laughed too loud, or blared lights unnecessarily. I eventually graduated to a managerial position, having much control and authority in overseeing several sites. The people I supervised perceived me as a disciplinarian, and I swiftly reprimanded one staff person when she denounced me for having a "very sharp tongue." In keeping to my need for personal routine, I further distanced myself from my fellow managers when I expressed unwillingness to personally cover hours caused by staff shortage and requested that they take on the added time, knowing that many were already covering extra hours. On another occasion I received a telephone call at home from a distraught member of staff to inform me that her brother had just been killed in an out-of-state car accident. She needed an immediate leave of absence and would be gone the rest of the week. My first reaction was to say, "You mean you're not coming in *at all?*" This was, of course, an appalling statement to make in her time of duress, but what I heard her say was that she wasn't coming to work, and I was focused on filling the void her absence would leave.

This type of reaction fuels the stereotype that people with autism and Asperger's are insensitive and incapable of being compassionate. As I've already said, I'm an intensely sensitive person. I'm just not always able to call up appropriate emotion *in the moment* without the opportunity to process it. As I've become more and more honest with myself about myself, I've been better able to be sensitive when it's warranted and sometimes even beyond that by relating the circumstances to myself. It all came in time as part of a maturation process. Sometimes, too, knowing the acceptable, diplomatic thing to say in the moment can be of immeasurable benefit, even if one doesn't feel it just then.

Let's then be mindful of the expectations we impose upon others in molding them into what we think they need to be. I'm not a social butterfly. I never will be, and *I don't want to be.* I don't want any more people in my life. I don't want any more friends than I've already got *unless I choose it.* I've never minded my own company. I've been bored, but rarely lonely. With no offense to anyone, it is unpleasant for me to have to "do" people for hours at a time. This is something many people don't understand, just as I don't understand those people who emphatically proclaim they'd go crazy if they didn't have others around them to talk to. I am so often intensely self-conscious that I also have great difficulty initiating conversation; it is easier to simply do nothing. My preference is to remain on the outer fringe as an observer, all the while secretly dying for someone else to make the first contact. While anyone can be willfully compelled and manipulated to meet our expectations, there is a breaking point at which rebellion reigns. Sometimes the best learning comes courtesy of the school of hard knocks, for all concerned.

Being in control is paramount for all people with Asperger's. Related to this is a need for predictable sameness in routines. If anything or anyone interferes with my personal schedule, I can become annoyed or even incensed. For example, I was recently in the car with a friend headed for the supermarket. En route, my friend said he needed to stop at K-Mart prior to the grocery (they are both in the same mall area). This was terribly distressing to me. Conversely, my friend thought the request a minor thing, and was perplexed when I told him I was upset because he didn't give me any advance notice in order to prepare for the detour. What he didn't realize was that, in my mind, going to the supermarket was a "done deal." In my head, I had already visualized going in, getting what I needed, and getting out. Conceptually, I was already back home, moving ahead to the next thing on my agenda.

For me, this need for sameness has extended to other areas. When it comes to my diet, I'm perfectly fine eating the same foods day in and day out. I've always been challenged by fashion. In junior high school, I thought one key to success was having lots of clothes regardless of whether they were in style or not. Rummaging through old bins in our attic, I discovered enough discards to supplement my present wardrobe. My appearance was odd because I attired myself in clothing that was outdated by at least a decade, such as shirts with antiquated prints or voluminous troubadour sleeves, and bright maroon corduroy trousers. By high school, I was buying *GQ*, the men's fashion magazine, in an attempt to emulate the male models. What I didn't realize was that the clothing presented therein was the very cutting edge of fashion, geared more toward trendy urbanites, and not high schoolers in suburban Pennsylvania. Eventually, I stopped bothering to show concern for clothes at all, preferring to stick with what I had until prompted to make an occasional acquisition by friends who would tell me I needed new clothes. Today, I still can't justify spending money on clothes and am comfortable going up to ten years at a time without buying anything. When I do make a purchase, it's to replace a garment that has become threadbare with a like item. I've also taken to wearing a lot of black because I feel comfortable and more confident in it. Black absorbs light, but, as my friend Jasmine tells me, black is also for disappearing (i.e. becoming inconspicuous), which is why magicians use it. Even now, I've continued to have a rather skewed perspective of what looks best, so it's easier to simply shroud myself in basic black.

Perhaps this need for sameness in routine and lifestyle also accounts for an area typical of many with Asperger's: lack of initiative and motivation. We can hold grand aspirations for our future but we're inadequate when it comes to the means to execute our plans. Our attempts to do so often fail because of our limitations and misunderstanding of the covert social code. Often too, our dreams don't mesh well with what others think is best for us. Thus, we find satisfaction, contentment or acquiescence in mediocrity, though we pine for more.

As is true of many folks with Asperger's, I've always had a very rigid sense of justice and injustice. I can't tolerate a liar, nor can I abide passive-aggressive behavior. If you don't like me, have the fortitude to say just that, I can deal with it because it's black and white. What I dislike intensely are people who are kind to me in person, but destructive and duplicitous behind my back. I never forget a kindness, but I also rarely forgive a slight. The cardinal rule in establishing trust with anyone, but particularly someone with Asperger's or autism, is *keep your promises.* Do what you say you're going to do when you say you're going to do it, and if not take the ownership of sincerely apologizing and offering an honest and legitimate excuse in a timely manner. If you are disingenuous, you will quickly move from my "A list" to another list – and you know what that list is. My general rule of thumb has been three strikes and you're out, but depending upon the person, it may be less than that. I have, quite unemotionally, cut people – friends, co-workers and my own mother – out of my life without regret or remorse for such offenses. Of course, the challenge is that all the time people say they're going to do things that they never have any intention of doing. How often do we hear people say "I'll call you," "Let's plan on getting together soon," or "Let's have lunch." These people are well intentioned and sincere, but they are speaking in a rhetorical sense that has become socially acceptable to many.

I have a younger brother whom I strongly suspect may also be Asperger's. As a child he was intensely passionate about collecting baseball cards, and could recite intricate statistics at will. He won numerous spelling bee awards, was mathematically adept and extremely willfull and headstrong in his thinking. He seemed to be interested in others for the value of what they could do for him. He also had very strong opinions about right and wrong. When my mother abandoned the family without warning, it was particularly devastating for him. He refused to see her, and eventually divorced himself from the family completely, even changing his name. Neither my family nor I have had contact with him in nearly twenty years, so final is his ostracism.

I see some of my traits in my own father, they're just more exaggerated in me. Recently, my grandmother (my father's mother) told me that my grandfather was not social, though he excelled in school dramatic productions. Once married, she supported him to become more outgoing and interactive. (Not surprisingly, in my work I'm prone to recognize the autism in family members, usually fathers, such that I see many children who come by their experience honestly.)

I'm next going to foray into an area of discussion that is controversial but absolutely necessary in supporting the whole person: sexuality. We are all sexual beings, but when we talk about caring for people with different ways of being, we'd rather not "go there" in our thinking. It becomes too much to consider in lieu of the additional services and supports we coordinate with or on behalf of an individual. Or it becomes too much to consider because of the stereo-typical perceptions of individuals as being asexual, unknowledgeable, or childlike. But to deny someone's sexuality is to presuppose the authority to regulate their humanity.

I've refrained from defining my own sexuality for the reader thus far because I didn't wish it to be a detractor. As early as three years old, I distinctly recall being possessed of a same sex attraction. As one might expect, at this early age I recall a strong fondness for certain fictional or comic strip characters with strong, dashing personas such as Captain

Hook, Mandrake the Magician or Popeye's Brutus. By four, I had a raging crush on Ron Ely as Tarzan in the 1967 television series. I said I didn't wish for this revelation to be a detractor because I do not want to provide my critics with the fodder to contend that my growing up experience was simply an unfortunate byproduct of my sexuality. In part, my growing up may have been influenced by my sexuality, but it certainly had nothing to do with the experiences of social awkwardness and indifference, and of being intrinsically constant in my thinking and personal habits. I am well aware of the challenges, hardships and prejudices endured by many youths of a same sex persuasion, but I've also known others with the same persuasion who have not shared these experiences, were popular, well liked, academically sound and athletic. What is curious is that I've learned that same sex attraction is not rare in men with Asperger's. Perhaps in some way it relates to the sense of safety in sameness and comfort in what is familiar. For me, the female form is so foreign that it is cold, alien and completely devoid of any sexual appeal. I don't feel any special allegiance to the gay community; to suggest that I should is like suggesting that one should feel obliged to collude with persons of the same eye color or nationality. Like my propensity for Asperger's, the same sex seed had simply been planted long before anyone's cognizance.

I have enjoyed two long-term relationships since leaving home at age eighteen (which precipitated my changing colleges), and a fleeting, tumultuous one with an emotionally insecure person who exerted a lot of control and referred to me as his "little mouse." At the time of writing, I am in the seventeenth year of my present relationship (fortunately, he's an accountant). It has been a growing and learning time for us both in adjusting to my personal sensitivities and limitations. In essence, I've never been on my own. I've always had a protector to support me in navigating through adult life. I stand in tremendous admiration of my Asperger's brothers who are making it on their own, struggling to support themselves and striving to achieve their life goals. For me, I know I would not be where I am now if it hadn't been for the consistent guidance and support.

Once I was able to forgive and release the haunting of my past and feel good about my life, I was able to once again embrace Oz without care (although I still do feel a twinge of embarrassment when people ask me about it). *The Wizard of Oz* came back to me tenfold as I experienced personal and professional growth and contentment. I am living proof of what it is to pursue one's passion. I have co-authored four successful books, including a deluxe pop-up book based on the MGM movie. (In collaborating with the book's paper engineers, I was thrilled to dialogue with a man who had worked on the 1968 Oz pop-up book – the very one I knew so well from the hours spent replicating it as a child!). I am co-owner of a large collection of Oz memorabilia (can you imagine life-size wax museum effigies of Judy Garland and company?). I have illustrated a *Wizard of Oz* board game, and was editor of a professional Oz journal for over five years. I've made numerous television appearances, and in spring 2000 my co-author and I were asked to lecture at the Library of Congress in conjunction with that institution's acclaimed Oz exhibition.

So often we expect people to be what we want them to be without realizing that they can never realistically hope to comply because it's what we want, not what they want. In fact the most important, powerful and respectful thing we could do is simply to ask "Are you happy?" or "What do you want?" We tend to shy away from asking the question "What do you want?" because we fear that people will ask for grandiose and extravagant things. I once facilitated a consultation for a young man in his twenties who was kind, bright and articulate, but who was repeatedly interrupted by others who felt the need to highlight his shortcomings. When I finally asked him, "What do you want?" he replied quite simply, "To just be accepted...but that would take a miracle." Don't we all just want to be accepted?

I will confide that on the edge of forty, I am self-diagnosed. This is not at all uncommon for people my age, older and slightly younger than I am. Asperger's Syndrome has only become recognized as a viable diagnosis within the past ten years or so. A friend of mine who is a psychiatrist has offered to provide me with the "official" diagnosis, but I've been too frugal to spring for the money it would cost. Perhaps it's that and a bit of procrastination. Coming to terms with and confronting the diagnosis has been a rather daunting prospect. The specter of the label looms before me. Do I approach it and extend an olive branch in an act of goodwill, or do I run like hell the other way?

In seeking some answers, I once attended an out-of-state autism conference where many of the presenters were autistic. I gingerly approached one man with Asperger's in the hopes of connecting. When I told him I was struggling in seeking resolve, his reply was to assert that his "radar" for detecting other "Aspies" (slang for Asperger's) was sounding, and that, at that moment, I was flashing all over his screen. While his response clearly demonstrated his bravura, it was not at all the sort of sensitive support I needed. How does one respond to such a statement? "Gosh, I'm sorry to be a blip on your radar screen. I hope I haven't been too much of a distraction."

Another psychiatrist provided me with some sage advice that I will not forget. As we've already acknowledged, any psychiatrist is vulnerable to whatever disclosures you choose to make. In essence, if you are determined to attain a certain diagnosis, it is largely possible. Thus, labels are subjective and perhaps personally unimportant. The psychiatrist advised that if the label "works," use it. And if at any time it stops working, I alone am empowered to surrender it, not surrender to it. I'd like to think that, for now, it's working. If it weren't, I don't know how I could conceive of doing what I do successfully. I have no formal background or training in autism. I work purely from intuition, drawing upon my own experience. My instincts *never* fail me. What I recommend that people do in my role as a consultant works. When I have a speaking engagement, I am universally well received and often invited back to the same locale two, three and four times. In fact, I have now deliberately determined *not* to seek a formal diagnosis as an advocate for the many adults also without diagnoses. At long last, so much of my life makes sense and I have found my calling. It is indeed an honor, and I am filled with an inner peace and tranquility. I have been very lucky in life and don't take any of it for granted, not for a moment. I see too many other people like me who are struggling to make a living, struggling to get by, struggling to just fit in. My life experiences pale in comparison, and if I had to relive my life knowing what I know now – knowing that I was going to be a messenger – I'd do it all over again in a minute. I'm so grateful for the opportunity to share good and great information endorsed by those with different ways of being. I'm grateful that people come and sit and listen to my sentiments of understanding and acceptance. And I will continue doing it so long as there are people who wish to hear it. Yes, I'd say that, for now, the label's working quite well, and for that I am humbly grateful.

Chapter 8

Team Building

Strong, collaborative teams are essential to successfully supporting the person with an autistic experience. Teams are usually comprised of parents and family members, caregivers, educators, case managers, service provider staff, doctors and therapists. When teams are unsuccessful in supporting those with different ways of being, it is due to inconsistency in philosophy, communication and actions. This directly impacts the degree of success the person experiences, such that when someone "fails," it is through no fault of their own.

The following scenarios are provided for the purpose of a team-building activity. Each participant should receive their own copy of the instructions and the scenarios. (Permission to reproduce the instructions and scenarios is granted.) Often, such group work is more productive and less emotionally threatening when a team can focus its attention and energies on a situation unknown and unfamiliar (but which may parallel a similar, real life situation).

It is helpful for more than one team to process each scenario concurrently, so that varying perspectives may be shared when reporting the findings. Thus it is best to divide into small groups in order to meet separately from one another, and then return to a large group for discussion purposes. I have found that each small group needs about twenty minutes to half an hour to complete each scenario. I strongly recommend reconvening for large group discussion *after each* small group scenario review. In other words, process each scenario separately and one at a time. One person should serve as a facilitator to guide the large group discussions.

The discussions about each scenario will be optimal if each participant has read this book, or, at the least, genuinely subscribes to person-centered philosophies. While discussing the outcomes is important, it is equally important to recognize the team-building process and group dynamics that occur during each discussion. There are no absolute answers; we must all listen to what each contributes to the discussion. Each team will likely generate far more questions than resolutions, but knowing the right questions to ask is of great value and time well spent.

In formulating responses, people's foremost inclination may be to fall back on what they already know. Make an effort to set those first reactions aside, and come back to them last. Begin to think more creatively and reflectively in unraveling the heart of the issues. The Guiding Principles listed at the end of the chapters should be of immeasurable benefit, and it may be helpful to post them visibly, or collate them as a handout for each participant. Above all else, allow the truth to guide you.

Instructions for teams supporting individuals with autism

You will be asked to carefully consider the scenario-specific situations with which you are presented. You are one member of a team, and will need to collaborate and communicate effectively and creatively with your team members. You are not necessarily charged with developing concrete resolutions. Supporting others is a dynamic process that may change over time as someone grows, acquires new skills, or develops other interests or passions. However, you will be asked to do the following:

1. Use a holistic, person-centered philosophy as the foundation for your work.

2. Brainstorm, strategize, deduce, and surmise potential recommendations based upon the person-specific information at hand. Prepare to report your recommendations.

3. Develop a list of questions about areas the team is considering, but about which there is incomplete information. How would requesting this information be useful or helpful for the team? What could be further explored once the information is provided?

4. Identify potential resources (natural and formal) that could support what someone experiences. How would you know if they are helpful or of use to the person?

5. Identify potential next steps in the process. What is needed to be in place in order to support the person fully and successfully? Where are opportunities for independence (i.e. control)?

6. Appoint a spokesperson for your group to report your findings.

In your work, you will not only consider what we are learning about people with autism; be mindful of the following areas:

- The person's diagnosis (is there more than one?).

- The person's medical history.

- The person's age.

- The person's current medication regime, and the reason for each prescription.

- Are there presently supports in place? Are they effective?

- What is the person's current mode of communication?

- What is a typical daily routine for the person?

- Does social or cultural diversity directly impact the situation?

Scenario # 1: Brock

Brock is a healthy eight-year-old boy diagnosed with autism and learning differences. He lives with his mother and six-year-old brother. Brock doesn't speak but does make vocalizations that sometimes sound like words. His mother usually understands him. For the past nine months or so, Brock has become self-abusive, banging his head against the wall or on the floor, as well as being aggressive toward others (i.e. kicking and throwing items at his family and his therapeutic aide). These incidents have resulted in injuries and some physical damage to the home and furnishings. Brock's pediatric psychiatrist has prescribed psychotropic medications to control these behaviors, but to date the psychiatrist has not found the right dosage or drug combination without Brock being sedated, and the behaviors continue. Brock currently takes 4 mg a day of Risperdal and 75 mg a day of Clozaril, both for anxiety and affect. The current medications seem to "slow him down" enough that the family can better function.

Brock attends a special education class at school with other children with learning differences. The classroom teacher and therapeutic aide are working on teaching Brock to use picture cards with illustrations and words on them in order to learn how to ask for help, to go to the bathroom, and to remain calm when the school bell rings. Brock seems to do better in school than at home, which is frustrating for his mother. She sometimes believes Brock's behavior is "her fault," or feels guilty because of the attention she must give Brock's younger brother. The therapeutic aide gets discouraged because she doesn't feel that Brock's mom is following through on the behavior plan they consented to.

Brock's grandmother saw something on TV about a new treatment that can cure autism in some children, and has been pressuring Brock's mother to travel to the next state to take Brock to a facility willing to try the new method. The grandmother is also very concerned for the safety of her six-year-old grandson.

Scenario #2: Stephanie

Stephanie is a twenty-seven-year-old woman who has short brown hair and big brown eyes. She is new to her group home, which she shares with two other women. Steph is diagnosed with autism, learning differences, and does not speak. Stephanie communicates by making screeching noises. She prefers to spend most of her time in the same spot on the sofa. When she isn't watching staff carefully, Stephanie uses her fingertips to press on her eyelids, sits and blinks, and then repeats the behavior. She will also suddenly jump up and start flapping her arms while screeching loudly. A behavior plan to terminate these behaviors is in the works.

Stephanie appears to enjoy pressing on her bladder and making herself urinate. This also occurs several times a day, and is not something that she did at the institution before coming to live at the community home three months earlier. Her staff have been told that Stephanie is probably feeling anxiety and is expressing herself through this behavior. Since it is hurting no one, the staff have been told that it's okay to allow for it at present, and to keep Stephanie clean and dry.

Stephanie enjoys music, and when country and western songs come on the radio, she puts her ear right up against the speaker. Staff then redirect her back to the sofa where she smiles and "sings" along.

Scenario #3: Ron

Ron is a thirty-one-year-old man with Asperger's Syndrome who lives alone in an apartment. Ron has a full-time job working in a computer store at the mall. Ron's co-workers often ask him to cover shifts when they want to take time off, or to mind the store when they want to take breaks together, which he does willingly. Other times, Ron's co-workers alternate asking Ron to have lunch in the food court, but then ask Ron to pay for their meals as well as his own.

Ron loves computers and relates well to them. His co-workers – and even his boss – frequently draw upon Ron's encyclopedic knowledge. He occasionally gets credit for his expertise. It is difficult for Ron to approach new customers without inundating them with too much information. He has come to look upon himself as "Mr Wrong." However, Ron majored in communications at college, and did exceptionally well in speech courses.

Ron has experienced severe depression in the past, and has a mental health case manager. When Ron was fifteen, he attempted suicide. Ron has been clear about wanting to explore other alternatives to medication for depression. Ron has been inconsistent or evasive with his case manager about taking his prescription of Prozac, which he says makes him feel nauseated.

Ron's parents are in their sixties, and live across town from him. They know that he was always considered "odd," but are also aware that he is very bright in certain areas and has always had a knack for fixing things. They are concerned about his future, particularly after they are gone. They are aware that he can be perceived as "gullible" and can be taken advantage of. They would like for Ron to be more social, date, and eventually settle down and marry. Ron seems disinterested in women, but has gone to the adult bookstore in town.

On his time off, Ron spends hours working on his computer in his apartment. Other times, he hangs out at the computer store where he works, but was recently asked not to come in except when he is scheduled to be there.

Scenario #4: Christina

Christina is a seventeen-year-old young woman diagnosed with autism. She attends a typical high school and is included in a regular classroom. In the past, Christina has been a target of verbal abuse by her peers, who have made her cry publicly on several occasions with their cruel words. She keeps to herself, and is considered "weird" by the other kids because she doesn't fit with any one group or clique. At lunchtime, Christina sits by herself and reads, or pets a stuffed mouse that she carries in her purse. Christina doesn't do well in gym class, especially with team sports. She does enjoy swimming though. She takes an interest in her personal appearance, and enjoys dressing in unique outfits and wearing her long blonde hair in different ways. Sometimes her peers consider her tastes to be eccentric but she is generally considered to be very attractive. Christina was close to one girl last year, but that person moved away, and they have lost touch.

Christina is a vegetarian, and is concerned with animal rights. She is also artistic and spends her free time drawing mice or writing poetry. Since getting her driver's license, she also enjoys going for rides by herself in the country or visiting a nearby farm, where she watches the cows and horses.

Christina's parents would like for her to consider going to college or art school but she doesn't indicate any interest or gets upset and cries when they broach the subject. They have also noticed her talking less and less. Christina would like to be able to continue living at home with her parents, creating more mouse drawings, and writing more poetry. She also dreams of falling in love with a handsome older man who will support her, devote himself to her completely, and be unconditionally accepting of her wants and needs.

Scenario #5: Jared

Jared is an attractive, healthy six-year-old boy with pervasive developmental disorder not otherwise specified (PPD NOS) who is fully included in his typical first grade class. He seems to have a limited vocabulary and when he speaks, it is usually in very soft tones. In class, he has an aide who sits next to him and helps to guide him through activities. Jared often appears to be distracted or deep in thought. At these times, his aide will move his chin to look at whatever requires his attention, or to look at her face while she speaks. Also, while Jared's teacher is talking, his aide gives him instructions to ensure he follows directions.

During group classroom activities, the pace is such that — even with support — Jared falls behind the instructions or becomes distracted. Sometimes, for no apparent reason, he makes noises out loud, or, when his aide is trying to be helpful, he reaches out and grabs her long hair or her dangling jewelry. When he does this, he is sent to "time out," which is a separate room outside his classroom. His aide escorts him, and, once there, she voices her expectation that he begin to work where the class left off. The time out room is self-contained, with white walls, overhead lighting and no window for distractions. Sometimes, when Jared is in the room, he hits his face.

Jared is very emotionally sensitive, loves elephants and submarines, and expresses his desire to his family that he wants to be in school with "the other children." His family perceives him as anxious or scared sometimes, and Jared tells them that, on occasion, he "sees" things.

Helpful hints for team facilitators

The following observations are intended for use *only* by the person facilitating large group team discussions. These observations should be shared after each small team has processed each scenario, and has reported their findings.

Scenario #1: Brock

- Do we know if Brock's diagnoses are accurate/current?

- Has thought been given to his communication methods?

- If Brock is trying to use speech, and his mother understands it, how is that valued and supported?

- What happened nine months ago?

- Where is Brock's father?

- Who are the medications helping?

- Is Brock's communication system at school effective *for him*?

- Is the family vested in the behavior plan?

- People have busy lives. Be mindful of what we are imposing on Brock's mother.

- Do we readily discount grandmother, or are there ways to engage her proactively?

Scenario #2: Stephanie

- How does Stephanie presently communicate (there are many, many ways)?

- How is she asserting personal control?

- What happens when you press on your own eyelids?

- Why do we think Stephanie presses on her bladder (seeking time with staff; control; sexual pleasure; safety in sameness and comfort in what is familiar)?

- How does Stephanie fill her time, and how could her passions be maximized?

- What do we know about Stephanie's staff and housemates?

Scenario #3: Ron

- Is Ron being taken advantage of at work?

- Who is going to tell a thirty-one-year-old man what he needs in his life?

- Is Ron still depressed, or is he bearing a sixteen-year-old label?

- If we were to offer Ron other vocational options, what might he best excel at?

- It what ways could Ron be social (be sure to explore computer possibilities)?

- Why doesn't Ron access adult bookstore material from his computer?

- What's the single most important question we could ask Ron? ("What do you want?" or "Are you happy?")

Scenario #4: Christina

- Christina is very clear in stating what she wants. How do we demonstrate that we value her communication?

- Is what Christina wants realistic?

- How can we best engage Christina, and value her wants?

- Who might be in the best position to demystify "college" for Christina?

- Is Christina completely devoid of self-esteem?

- If college is not an option, what are other areas to be explored?

Scenario #5: Jared

- In what ways is Jared not fully respected?

- What could Jared's classroom teacher and aide do differently?

- Is the aide's expectation of Jared upon reaching the time out room helpful?

- Is the time out room unnecessarily punitive?

- Do all children use this particular time out room?

- What is Jared saying he wants?

- What is meant by "on occasion he 'sees' things?"

Instructions for teams supporting individuals with autism and mental health experiences

You will be asked to carefully consider the scenario-specific situations with which you are presented. You are one member of a team, and will need to collaborate and communicate effectively and creatively with your team members. You are not necessarily charged with developing concrete resolutions. Supporting others is a dynamic process that may change over time as someone is supported in ways that demonstrate we are learning about others' unique experiences, and are pursuing a whole person approach that includes proactive clinical treatment. However, you will be asked to do the following:

1. Use the framework for identifying mood disorders in persons with autism (found in Chapter 6) as the foundation for your work. Be prepared to also consider issues of trauma and anxiety. Remember:

   ○ People have good reasons for doing what they do

   ○ they are doing the very best they know how to *in the moment.*

2. Brainstorm, strategize, deduce, and surmise potential recommendations based upon the person-specific information at hand. Prepare to report your recommendations.

3. Develop a list of questions about areas the team is considering, but about which there is incomplete information. What questions could be asked of the people who know the person best? What questions could be asked of the person's psychiatrist? How would requesting this information be useful or

helpful for the team? What could be further explored once the information is provided?

4. Rule in or rule out the potential for mood disorder, trauma, and/or anxiety. What are the symptoms (*not* behaviors)? How do you justify the symptoms as fitting the criteria for a mood disorder? Are there clusters of symptoms present?

5. Identify potential next steps in the process. What is needed to be in place in order to support the person fully and successfully?

6. Appoint a spokesperson for your group to report your findings.

In your work, you will not only consider what we are learning about people with autism and mental health experiences; be mindful of the following areas:

- The person's diagnosis (is there more than one?).

- The person's medical history.

- The person's age.

- The person's current medication regime, and the reason for each prescription.

- Are there presently supports in place? Are they effective?

- What is the person's current mode of communication?

- What is a typical daily routine for the person?

- Does social or cultural diversity directly impact the situation?

Scenario #1: Allan

Allan is a nineteen-year-old young man with autism and learning differences who is also diagnosed with obsessive-compulsive disorder and intermittent explosive disorder. His psychiatrist has prescribed him Risperdal, 3 mg twice a day, Mellaril, 50 mg twice a day, and Ativan, 2 mg twice a day. Allan does not speak and those who know him would say he communicates through "behaviors." Allan lives in a foster care home, and his houseparents are the third such family to care for him after he was placed out of his natural mother's home at age four. The little information that is known about his mother indicates that she abused drugs and alcohol.

Allan has a long reputation for violent, difficult-to-manage behaviors requiring physical restraints, and which have included three psychiatric hospitalizations. The hospitalizations were ultimately not helpful and Allan was discharged quite sedated. He has also been through five behavior plans, but nothing is effective.

His current houseparents are exhausted by his "acting out" behaviors, and, together with Allan's school district, the team is actively seeking placement for Allan in an out-of-state autism center where he will be better managed. At times, and especially on weekends or holidays, Allan will pace through the house for hours, or will engage in obsessive-compulsive behaviors such as banging open and shut his bedroom door, and rocking in a rocking recliner so hard he has broken two such chairs. In fact, when he is denied these activities, his behavior escalates and he can become violent. In the past year, Allan has pulled his housemother's hair and broken her finger. She said that, during the assault,

Allan was laughing and seemed to "enjoy it." On another occasion, Allan raised his fist as if to strike his housefather, but instead he shattered a kitchen window, for which he required stitches. He has been known to climb on the top of sofas and counters, and jump off them with his arms outstretched. Once he seriously cut his forehead doing this. After these periods of time pass, Allan has openly wept or moaned, and has attempted to hug those he has injured. He then goes into a "shut down" phase, and cannot be coaxed from his room for several days.

Scenario #2: Brett

Brett is a twenty-three-year old man with Asperger's Syndrome who lives alone in an apartment. He received his diagnosis two years ago. Brett has always preferred being alone to read about astronomy, or, when he was a boy, spending time with his grandfather on his grandfather's farm. This occurred every weekend until Brett's grandfather died when Brett was twelve years old.

When Brett was fifteen, he was sexually assaulted by three older teenage boys, who inserted the handle of a broom into his rectum. Treatment in the hospital and being questioned by police were very confusing times for Brett. No one could understand – not even his parents – why he didn't just run away, or call for help instead of doing what the boys told him to do "because they were older" than he was. The boys involved lied about the assault, and said that it was "fooling around" (i.e. consensual) because Brett complied with it. The boys were placed on probation, but Brett still had to confront them every day in school until he dropped out in his junior year to work at K-Mart stocking shelves. He still works at K-Mart doing the same job.

Brett's co-workers would describe him as dependable, quiet and shy, but sometimes moody or irritable. About once a year, Brett complains of sharp pains in his chest and calls off sick for several days. No medical doctor can find any cause for Brett's pain, and it is concluded that it is psychosomatic. Also, during these times, Brett goes without eating, preferring to just stay in bed. When he does return to work, everyone comments on his weight loss, which makes him even more self-conscious. Sometimes, Brett makes nicks in his flesh with a pocketknife to the point of drawing blood.

Scenario #3: Jonathon

Jonathan is a fourteen-year-old young man diagnosed with pervasive developmental disorder not otherwise specified (PPD NOS), mild learning differences and schizoaffective disorder. Jonathan always seemed to have lots of energy, but within the past year he has been described as especially intense and even "out of control." This kind of "wild" behavior usually occurs about every other month, and for his disorder he is prescribed high doses of Risperdal, Cogentin, and Zyprexa. However, to date, nothing has worked, so Jonathan's psychiatrist keeps adjusting the doses or adding new medications.

When Jonathan meets with his psychiatrist, he demands that she call him "Captain Crunch." He seems to delight in explaining that he intends to marry her in order to rape her and make an army of "Crunch-babies" to take over the world. He has also made similar statements to his mother and seventeen-year-old sister, while laughing and smiling with a "fake" sounding evil laugh.

Jonathan is passionate about Nascar racing, and during his "out of control" times, he will want to watch Nascar videos over and over again. Once, when his father insisted that Jonathan turn off the TV, Jonathan threw it across the room and screamed loudly in a "different" voice that he was going to kill his dad. Other times, Jonathan will be moving around in his room most of the night, and, in the morning, will tell his family stories about the space aliens that came into his room. In the next breath, Jonathan will change the subject and talk about Nascar. Then he will quickly shift to talking about the Crunch-babies again.

Although he has threatened physical violence against others, Jonathan has only broken lamps, vases, or knocked pictures off walls. Once, during such an incident, he cut himself badly on a ceramic shard and it is unclear if he did this intentionally or not. Two years ago, Jonathan went through a period in which he talked a lot about fatal diseases, would skip meals saying he was ill, and, in general, seemed to "slow down."

Bibliography

The following is a list of resources I like best because they have been useful and practical, and subscribe to respectful, humanistic philosophies.

A is for Autism. Princeton, NJ: Films for the Humanities & Sciences, Inc. (1-800-257-5126), 1992.
This beautiful, brief film is animated, scored and narrated by people speaking to their autistic experiences. It is mandatory viewing for anyone in human services.

Ball, M.S. (1999) *Kiss of God: The Wisdom of a Silent Child*. Deerfield Beach, FL: Health Communications.
Neither autism nor Marshall Ball's use of facilitated communication are defined as such, but this book has become a personal touchstone for me. Marshall's written thoughts and poetry are nothing less than exquisite and thought provoking.

Cohen, S. (1998) *Targeting Autism*. Berkeley: University of California Press.
A generally fair and balanced perspective of autism and intervention approaches and supports.

Grandin, T. (1995) *Thinking in Pictures and Other Reports from My Life with Autism*. New York: Doubleday.
Expert personal testimony and insight from the leading autism self-advocate.

Gray, C. (1994) *The Original Social Story Book*. Arlington, TX: Future Horizons.
Primer for the best way I know to support others in feeling safe, comfortable and prepared for what to expect and what is expected in social situations.

Hill, D. A. and Leary, M.R. (1993) *Movement Disturbance: A Clue to Hidden Competencies in Persons Diagnosed with Autism and Other Developmental Disabilities.* Madison, WI: DRI Press.
A fascinating treatise that deconstructs and demystifies movement in folks with neurological differences.

Willey, L. Holliday (1999) *Pretending to be Normal: Living with Asperger's Syndrome.* London: Jessica Kingsley Publishers.
The book that clinched it for me. If ever I had any prior doubts about my own experience, this volume offered affirmation. Liane Holliday Willey relates a pivotal event (one of her daughters was diagnosed with Asperger's) that led to her adult journey of self-discovery and personal reflection.

Kephart, B. (1998) *A Slant of Sun: One Child's Courage.* New York: W.W. Norton.
Beth Kephart's elegant prose tells of boundless mother's love in her quest for understanding and appreciating the unique beauty within her son.

Moyes, R.A. (2001) *Incorporating Social Skills in the Classroom: A Guide for Teachers and Parents of Children with High-Functioning Autism and Asperger's Syndrome.* London: Jessica Kingsley Publishers.
A straightforward, functional, and very readable handbook for care-givers and educators with lots of anecdotes, examples, and makes-sense strategies to support learning and social interaction.

O'Neill, J.L. (1999) *Through the Eyes of Aliens: A Book About Autistic People.* London: Jessica Kingsley Publishers.
Jasmine Lee O'Neill shares her wisdom, sound advice, poetry and artwork in writing of her own autistic experience.

Pary, R.J., Levitas, A.S. and Hurley, A. DesNoyers (1999)
"Diagnosis of bipolar disorder in persons with developmental disabilities." *Mental Health Aspects of Developmental Disabilities 2,* 2, April/May/June.
A clinical supplement to much of the information addressed in Chapter 6 of this book.

Index

sensory sensitivities, allowing for,
58–59, 70
social outs, 75–77, 81
visual thinkers-learners, 23, 36, 60–62,
80, 136
Leary, Martha, 84
light sensitivity, 92
listening, guiding principles for good, 16,
19, 20
literal interpretation, 26–27
Little Mermaid, 29
loss, sensitivity to, 104

males, greater likelihood of autism
among, 116
mania, symptoms of, 105–8
see also bipolar disorder
medication, 166
alternatives to, 111
antidepressants, 110
antipsychotic drugs, 110
effects of, 155
mood stabilizing, 110–11
psychotropic, 155
Men are From Mars, Women are from Venus,
116
mental health issues
anxiety, 101, 112, 115
autism, not medicated, 100, 115
control, loss of, 102–3, 115
family history and presence of cycles,
103, 115
guiding principles for, 115
love, power of, 114, 115
mental illness
equal opportunities offender,
99–100
misdiagnosis of, 100, 115
as undiagnosed, 100, 109–10, 115
mood disorders (see bipolar disorder)
post traumatic stress disorder, 101,
112–13, 115, 122–23
self-advocacy, 113, 115
self-knowledge, 114, 115
stereotypes, dispelling, 99–100
symptoms, problem of self-reporting,
101

mental retardation, shattering stereotype
of, 16
mood disorders *see* bipolar disorder
Moran, Barbara, 23, 40, 117
motivation, lack of, 143
movement see body movements
movie talk
acting opportunities, encouraging,
31–32, 132–33
practical application of, 30–31
reservations, addressing, 32–33
valuing as a strength, 28–30, 44
Moyes, Becky, 124
music, and reciprocal interaction, 33–34

noise sensitivity, 90–91

Obsessive-Compulsive Disorder (OCD),
83, 166
definition of, 72–73
passions seen as, 47–48, 51, 72–73
and perseverative activity, 72–75
O'Neill, Jasmine Lee, 47, 117, 143

pain
effect on behavior, 85–86, 94, 97
medical causes for, 99
parents, as partners, 18–19, 20
Parkinson's disease, 83
passions
age-appropriateness, 50–51, 120,
130–31
as bridge to social interactions, 47,
51–53, 57
depression, and loss of interest in, 104
guiding principles for valuing, 57
intensification of, as symptom of mania,
107
keeping alive, 50–51, 130–31
as learning opportunities, 48, 57, 59
misinterpretation of, 53–55, 57
not obsessive-compulsive disorder,
47–48, 51, 72–73
presenting to others, 53, 57
recognizing, 11–12, 46–47
rewards, avoiding using as, 49
symbolic meaning of, 54, 55–56